InBetween Sequels

Emotionally You
An Epic of Feelings... Created

By

Cassandra Huff

ISBN: 978-0-7596-4901-9 (sc)
ISBN: 978-0-7596-4900-2 (e)

Print information available on the last page.

This book is printed on acid-free paper.

1stBooks – rev. 06/27/24

PREFACE

EMOTIONALLY YOU... AN EPIC OF FEELINGS...CREATED
EMOTIONS CAN BE POSITIVELY EXPERIENCING...
JOURNEYING OVER AND BEYOND...
IN TOUCH WITH GLIMPSES OF
THE TRUTH... FEELINGS
DEFINED IN WORDS THAT STIR AN
AWAKENESS...

INTRODUCTION

EMOTIONALLY YOU... AN EPIC OF FEELINGS...CREATED

Emotions defined...

When dealing with the psychology of the mind... emotions then are falsehoods and/or truths that stir (arouse) a feeling of either insecurities or securities that create actions in and out of us which are either inhibiting or uplifting (enriching) in nature and serve as vehicles to help us progress or either digress to a healthy and/or unhealthy state of conscious awareness, hence conscious existence.

emotionalism...dramatism...evocatively...emotionally you...

Some writings written by Cassandra have been revised and appear in unpublished books she has authored.

Cassandra shares writings by her children, Kassinda, Kameelah, and Dennis II.

In their writings, feelings and thoughts of her and her children awakening to a greater evolvement are captured.

Cassandra lives in Decatur, Georgia with two of her children and, dog Kirby.

Her oldest daughter attends Georgia Tech, Atlanta, Georgia.

Kameelah attends Cedar Grove High School, Dennis II attends Avondale Elementary Magnet School for Performing Arts.

Quietly in an emotional whirlwind, the manifestation of a state of delusion and obsequiousness searching for a way of life that would bring contentment to her souls journey, Cassandra finds herself journeying through uneventful relationships. She searches deeply into herself writing countlessly of the love she yearns for. Not aggressively, however bravely she intensely examines her psychological being beckoning for her gentle spirit to be heard.

In Between Sequels
…Emotionally You An Epic
of Feelings…Created.

TABLE OF CONTENTS

Forgiving Pain

When you want to be left alone
I can't hear your pain or listen
it's because you don't want to share your pain...
for some reason you feel like pain should
not be shared,
I want too to be left alone but sometimes
I want only to be left alone with you.
Forgivingly, LISTEN and FEEL my Pain,
Can't you hear my pain.
The suffering of the world "others" is upon MY
shoulders, it seems, as if upon your shoulders too.
I don't understand.
Alone we-together-could be to share each other's pain.
My pain will ease and eventually leave one day... Yours Too!
Alone for long I choose not.
I want to be alone with you.
Bye, Bye for now you can be alone,
for you desire not to share what seems to be your endless pain.
A Blissful state will soon be attained.
I want to be with you.
Something Is Missing, It's You — Ease My Pain.

HAVING FAITH

BE PATIENT!

LISTEN!

TRUST!

HAVE FAITH!

A GENTLEMAN AT LAST

MY PURSE HE THREW OVER HIS SHOULDERS.
THE CAR DOOR HE OPENED - FOR ME!
THE PATIENT RESERVE OF A REAL GENTLEMAN.
CHIVALRY IT'S HERE!
"CAN I GET YOU ANYTHING, MAYBE SOMETHING TO DRINK",
He asked politely.
A GENTLEMAN - AT LAST - A DIVINE FEELING OF TRUTH.
A PEACEFUL, QUIET REPOSE - AT LAST A GENTLEMAN.
THE HONESTY AND SINCERITY IN THE WORDS THAT HE SPOKE
I KNOW A GENTLEMAN - AT LAST.
THE CONCERN, THE CARE, THE WARMTH —
THAT FEELING - GOSH
DON'T LET IT PASS.
IN MY LIFE A GENTLEMAN (HAS ARRIVED) AT LAST.

RED BIRD, RED BIRD

RED BIRD, RED BIRD HOW MAGICAL ARE YOU.
I WAS TOLD ALL I HAD TO DO WAS MAKE A WISH,
AND BLOW YOU A KISS, AND ALL OF MY DREAMS WOULD
COME TRUE.

SHOW ME RED BIRD, RED BIRD... HOW MAGICAL ARE YOU.
I HAVE MADE A WISH... I HAVE BLOWN YOU A KISS...
SHOW ME RED BIRD, RED BIRD...
MAKE ALL OF MY DREAMS COME TRUE.

RED BIRD, RED BIRD... SHOW ME... HOW MAGICAL ARE YOU.

TOUGH TIMES

-rolled them pennies.
-they carried us through.
-roll these pennies.
-they will carry us through.
-these pennies will buy us gas, oil, and bread if we need them (these pennies) to.
-all this metal - copper- the meaning behind we must know.
-copper (this penny) a tough precious metal (CU).
-copper its spiritual value goes unknown. for it supplies strong energy to body
 and mind, and it is said to raise self esteem.
-copper its medicinal value, I know it to be true, it will help diminish arthritic
 pain, rid impurities, and revitalize your energies.
-these pennies are made of copper and they will carry us through.
-its color reddish brown (penny), you are tough.
-surround us with this copper, it has helped us to maintain balance, and I know these
 pennies have definitely carried us through..

... WE MEET ...

FROM MY OFFICE DOOR HE PEERED IN AT ME,
AND RESPECTFULLY SAID MY NAME.
HIS AURA, AN ILLUMINATED WHITE LIGHT, TO
MYSELF I SAID AN ELEVATED MIND HAS HE.
AND THERE HE STOOD LOOKING AT ME
AS IF FOREVER WE'D KNOWN EACHOTHER...
FOREVER...
I DIDN'T KNOW IF I SHOULD GIVE HIM A HUG,
S-O-O, INDEED HIS HAND INSTEAD I SHOOK...
HE THEN TOOK A SEAT AND WE BEGAN TO STARE,
AS IF WE COULD NOT BELIEVE,
FINALLY WE MEET...
IN CONTROL I REMAINED FOR MY EMOTIONS I
DID NOT WANT TO SHOW...
AFTER ALL THESE MONTHS... WE MEET...
SO IDEAL WAS HIS CALIBER...
I KNOW HE IS FOR REAL...
MY IDEAL, WE FINALLY MEET...

always
"Cassandra"

Grandaddy

You were here with us for 87 years your industrious mind left
me with an entrepreneurial spirit..
I always wondered how many appliances had you repaired in your lifetime...
what I will remember mostly of you is yours and grandma Lou's loving
concern of what we wanted to be
what tickled me mostly is you laughing when I told you Uncle T.Z. ate his
grits with a butter knife
and what you meant by women with "schoolgirl shapes",
when it was time for you to put down the bottle and not light a cigarette,
it seems as if you did both without a quiver in your bone,
The physical body you inhabited chose not to house your soul any longer.
the time came for you to leave.
Your presence will always be.
The song Oh! Freedom lets me know that you truly are free to go.

Grandaddy you will always be loved.
"William Henry Huff" Uncle Son.
  "Nece"

Nakeah

You can soar, you can fly to heights unknown. As I sit and watch you receive your academic diploma tears flow down my cheeks.

Nakeah, I know what the struggles have been. Your mother, she did it all by herself-no help did she receive. The times I rocked you on my lap when I myself was with child, these decisions we choose in life, though sometimes we know not why. And then while in graduate school, I rocked both you and your cousin Kassinda, my colleagues helped to rock you too.

I know the wisdom and knowledge is there for while I read, I read to you... We made it, Nakeah, you can soar, you can fly, I know making it is in you. The nights your mother had to decide - the latch key syndrome had to be, a latch key kid we all created.

Your mother with thoughts of the lives of others did not want to interfere. So, your struggles Auntie does know. See it was all up to her to provide for you and make sure you had the necessities. And then I watched you struggle to be a responsible sister to your brother 12 years a part.

Your artistic creativity and your voice so sublime I surely hope in the darkness you will not let them lie. We all endured and your Papa too, for the days you thought not to make it to school, he made this possible for you. It was during these times we all realized just what we all had to do. Nakeah, you can soar, you can fly

Cedar Grove High School - Dekalb County- June 10, 1997

FALSE REALITY

YOU WORK AND DON'T GET PAID, WHY BECAUSE YOU SAY HE'S GIVING YOU
A CHANCE TO BE WHO YOU COULD NOT BE OUT IN SOCIETY.
IS THIS WHAT I AM TO BELIEVE.
WHAT COULD THIS BE- WHAT I'M HEARING IS THIS IS
YOUR FALSE REALITY. THIS IS YOUR EXISTENCE AND
YOU KNOW NO OTHER WAY TO BE.
WHAT DO YOU OWE HIM TO SIT AND NOT BE PAID.
HOW ARE YOUR BILLS PAID, HOW WILL YOU ARRIVE BY BUS OR CAR.
WHO BUYS YOUR BARE NECESSITIES- YOU KNOW THE
TOILET TISSUE AND SOAP TO BATH,
DON'T FORGET THE LOAF OF BREAD AND DOZENS OF EGGS IF THAT IS WHAT YOU EAT.
IS HE AN EMPLOYER THAT PROVIDES THESE LIBERALLY.
HOW ABOUT SOME FRUIT AND A LITTLE WINE ALONG THE WAY.
AND WHAT ABOUT THE TREATS TO YOURSELF ALL OF WHICH TAKE PAY.
YOU HAVE TO WORK - WHILE I WORK, PLEASE LET ME BE PAID. I DO VOLUNTEER
SERVICE SOMEWHERE ELSE.
NO ONE ELSE DO I OWE A THING; THIS IS WHAT I OWE MYSELF.
A MOVIE OR TWO, A GOOD BOOK TO READ, TO KEEP THE MIND STIMULATED.
THIS FALSE REALITY OF WORK AND NOT GET PAID HOW COULD YOU ALLOW
SOMEONE TO SIMULATE.
EVERY MAN SHOULD BE PAID ACCORDING TO HOW HE HAS LABORED, OF COURSE
ALL OF THE OTHER CREDENTIALS ADD TO THE NEST.
I WORK TO BE PAID AND CHOOSE NOT TO BE INVOLVED IN THIS

.FALSE REALITY.

Cassandra Huff

My inspiration:

*But let there be spaces in your togetherness, and let the winds of the
heavens dance between you.
Love one another, but make not a bond of love:
Let it rather be a moving sea between the shores of your souls.
Fill each other's cup but drink not from one cup.
Give one another of your bread but eat not from the same loaf.
Sing and dance together and be joyous, but let each one of you be alone,
Even as the strings of a lute are alone though they quiver with the same music
Give your hearts, but not into each other's keeping. For only the hand of
life can contain your hearts. And stand together yet not too near together:
For the pillars of the temple stand apart, and the oak tree and the cypress
grow not in each other's shadow.*

Prophet Kahlil Gibran

WE DON'T KNOW DEFEAT

LOOK TO THE HILLS FROM WHENCE YOUR HELP COMETH
TOGETHER WE WILL...

IT IS WITHIN OUR FAMILY WHERE WE CAN BE WHO WE REALLY ARE WHERE WE
DON'T KNOW DEFEAT. DARE NOT SHOW OUR TRUE SELF, NOT TO THE PUBLIC
ESPECIALLY FOR TRULY DEFEAT WE WILL SURELY MEET.
PUT ON THOSE MANY DIFFERENT FACES NOT YOUR REAL PERSONALITY

FOR IT IS WITHIN OUR FAMILY WHERE WE CAN BE WHO WE REALLY ARE WITHIN
OUR FAMILY WE KNOW NO DEFEAT.

JOBS EASY RELATIONSHIPS

A JOB IS JUST LIKE A RELATIONSHIP, KIND OF IN SOME WAYS.
listen OKAY! WE'VE COME TO CROSS(ING) ROADS HERE
LET'S EXAMINE NEW GOALS, TRADE OFFS, NEW OUTLOOKS, NEW
POSITIONS, WHAT WENT WRONG, WHERE DO THE DIFFERENCES LIE,
OOPS! END OF ROAD HERE.
THINK WE'D BETTER SEVER THOSE TIES
WE SEEM NOT TO BE IN SINK IN SOME WAYS ANYMORE
OKAY SOMETHING'S NOT CLICKING
WELL ONE THING IS DIFFERENT IN A (RELATIONSHIP) JOB ESPECIALLY
IF YOU DON'T HAVE A CONTRACT... YOU KNOW LIKE A MARRIAGE
RELATIONSHIP OR AN ENTREPRENEURIAL RELATIONSHIP CONTRACT.
LOOK, I'M GIVING MY 30 DAY NOTICE AND AFTER THAT WELL
BYE BYE JUST SEND ME ALL THAT'S DUE ME BY WAY OF MAIL,
NO NEED TO ASK QUESTIONS, NO NEED TO CALL,
AND OH! UHM! THANKS FOR THE EXPERIENCES IN THIS HERE JOB
(RELATIONSHIP).
WHY NOT BECOME A WORK ALOHOLIC
I MEAN REALLY JOBS ARE EASY WORK (RELATIONSHIPS).
JOBS ARE EASY RELATIONSHIPS.

mY pRIDE iS uP

mY pRIDE iS uP, I CAN'T FALL.
  THE FAITH IN MY EYES KEEPS ON GOIN AND YOU
  CAN'T HOLD ME BACK CAUSE OF MY PRIDE.
MY MAMA TELLS ME THAT YOU HAVE TO REACH YOUR GOAL,
YOUR GOAL WON'T REACH YOU.
  THE FAITH IN MY EYES KEEPS ON GOIN AND YOU CAN'T
HOLD ME BACK CAUSE OF MY PRIDE.
  WHY DOES THIS HAPPEN TO ME YOU CAN'T HOLD ME DOWN CAUSE
WHAT I HAVE IS TO MUCH TO BREAK DOWN.
NOW WHY DO YOU KEEP ON TRYING TO BREAK ME DOWN.
  IT WON'T HAPPEN, MY PRIDE IS UP, I CAN'T FALL.
IT'S A PART OF LIFE THAT'S WHAT SHE TOLD ME. EVERY NIGHT I GO TO
SLEEP I PRAY THAT TOMMORROW WILL BE A BETTER DAY AND THAT MY
PRIDE BEING UP IT WILL CONTINUE TO STAY.

Kameelah Densua Jahi Williams

fRIENDS

fRIENDS TO THE END MORE THAN GREAT MORE THAN
SAD. OUR TIMES GO ON FOREVER . FIRST TIME WE
MET WE KNEW THAT WE WERE FRIENDS TO THE END.

NOW THAT WE ARE FRIENDS, I GUESS BEST FRIENDS,
EACH NIGHT, EACH DAY, WE PRAY FOR EACHOTHER,
OUR PRAYERS ARE THAT WE DO NOT GET CAUGHT UP IN
THE WICKEDNESS OF SOCIETY.
IF YOU DON'T CALL THAT FRIENDS, I DON'T KNOW WHAT
ELSE TO CALL IT, FRIENDS TO THE END IS WHAT WE ARE.

kAMEELAH dENSUA jAHI wILLIAMS

'IT IS HE'

Though he came to this earthly plane with an affliction that could be deadly, he has a lot of good in him, why the streets he got caught up in, nobody really knows.

The brother that I know he has, perceives this good in him and though often he is a burden out of true love this brother cannot shun his blood.

The love his brother has for him is unique and meek and therefore you cannot help but sense his sincere care.

Though over his mind he has no control, there is nothing that he would not do for you... he has a heart as good as gold...many know this of him and for long cannot treat him cold.

This affliction that he came here with remains today all perhaps he does not receive, for his affliction, the treatment in need.

Regardless of this affliction in tune with GOD he must be, for he is blessed to be wise and has a gift to see... so as he roams from here to there in GODS hand is his safety you can rest assuredly.

We all have a purpose in life, some do not understand the experiences we must sometimes endure and it is not for another to judge or condemn.

Do not let me forget to mention his buddies.

For without them many days you cannot keep him in line and this is not said invain.

To understand him is what he needs and his brother understands in deed.

He keeps you laughing that's for sure. A lot of fun he can be, for he is definitely trip city.

His inner wisdom is what keeps him from meeting his fate, and for this reason he remains today with his family.

Everyone in the neighborhood and all around town knows him as 'IT IS HE', this is one person they don't mind calling on for he has an expertise in carpentry... when his affliction is not burdening most anything he can build and repair, and it is during these moments that he does his work with skill and care.

always
Cassandra

PAPA

MY FAVORITE PERSON IS MY PAPA
I LOVE HIM AND HE IS SPECIAL TO ME
HE HELPS ME WITH MY HOMEWORK
AND HE LOVES ME GENUINELY
HIS EYES CHANGE COLORS
IN THE DARK THEY ARE SO PRETTY
MY PAPA IS LIKE A LOLLY POP
SO SWEET AND GOOD TO ME.

KAMEELAH DENSUA JAHI WILLIAMS

VAMPIRE

ONCE A UPON A TIME THERE WAS A LITTLE GIRL NAMED
LIZA. IT WAS 10:00 P.M. AT NIGHT, SHE WAS AT THE LAKE
AND IT WAS A QUIET NIGHT AND YOU COULD HEAR FOOT
STEPS IN THE WOODS.
LIZA WAS SCARED, SOMETHING JUMPED OUT AND THAT
SOMETHING SAID SHH! AND SHE SAW 4 SHARP TEETH AND
SHE SAW BLOOD ON ITS TEETH, IT HAD GREEN EYES.
STAY AT HOME AT NIGHT UNLESS YOU ARE WITH A
RESPONSIBLE PERSON BECAUSE YOU DON'T KNOW WHAT
IS OUTSIDE THAT CAN SCARE AND HARM YOU.

KAMEELAH DENSUA JAHI WILLIAMS

BE BLACK

BE BLACK, BE BLACK

HOW DO YOU BE BLACK

TELL ME SO I'LL KNOW

BE BLACK, BE BLACK

TELL ME HOW TO BE BLACK

ALL I KNOW IS I HAD A BLACK DADDY AND A BLACK MOMMY TOO

THIS BE BLACK TELL ME HOW TO BE

IS THIS A RACE OR AN ETHNICITY

IS THIS A COLOR, AN ACTION, A CULTURE, OR A RACE TO ETERNITY

WHAT IS IT - HOW DO YOU BE BLACK

The Unveiling of Nece

"ISIS"

I AM ISIS THE GODDESS OF GODDESSES
I AM ISIS THE QUEEN OF QUEENS
I AM ISIS THE MOTHER OF PURITY
I AM THE GODDESS OF FERTILITY
   THE MOTHER OF JESUS...OF MUHAMMAD... OF BUDDHA...
   OF THE ADAM... OF ALL.
IN ALL MY WAYS THAT I SOW IS (ISIS)
  THAT I SAY IS (ISIS), I AM ALL.
I AM ISIS WHO CIVILIZED EGYPT...
  THE FIRST AND THE LAST.
THE VIRTUOUS ONE, THE IMMACULATE ONE.
I AM EVERY WOMAN/FEMALE (IN GOOD (GODLY) FORM)
THAT WAS, HAS BEEN, IS, AND IS TO BE.
  TIS WHAT IS (ISIS), I AM "ISIS" CAN'T YOU SEE.

I AM THAT I AM
S   S

ISIS

INTELLIGENT, INTUNE, INURE, INUNDATE, INTELLECTUAL,
 INCLUSIVE, INSPIRING, INSIGHTFUL, INSURING,
 INTUITIVE, INGENIOUS, IMPECCABLE

SOMETHING, SUBSTANCED, STATURED, SEGACIOUS, SINCERE, SONNET

IMMUTABLE, ILLUMINE, IMMORTAL, IMPERIAL, IRIDESCENT,
 INQUISTIVE, INVOCATIVE, IMMOVABLE, IMMACULATE, INVOLUTE

SUPREME, SERENE, STANDARD, SOLID, SPECIAL, SUMPTUOUS, SUPERIOR.

ISIS

The Woman

the woman can do anything she wants to do.
the woman can go out and get any job she wants to.
it does not matter if it's a mans job.
if the woman fights with all her might, she gets what she wants.
I PERSONALLY THINK THAT THE WOMAN CAN GET ANYTHING AND ALL SHE WANTS IF SHE PUTS HER MIND TO IT.

Kameelah Densua Jahi Williams

"The Story of My Life"

Well I live without my dad now.
I did get through it, so I do not cry anymore.
I will see him sometimes, sometimes I wish
he was here but there is no more pain to go through.
He made a decision that my mom could not accept,
she told us sometimes people grow apart,
that everyone is on a personal journey, and sometimes
we must go our own separate way.
I'll enjoy him when I see him, I'll continue to wish
him well, for if my mommy can let go, and no longer
be in pain, then I can too and we will all stand to gain.

Kameelah Densua Jahi Williams

My Glory

My glory, My glory, My glory.
How could this be.
I searched - prayed that the right one would arrive.
At him I looked feeling of course maybe he's the one.
Oh! the years have gone by and I wonder did I act to quickly.
My glory, My glory, My glory.
How could this be.
Is this GOD telling me after all these years he is not the one.
With Valor I go forth, Undaunted I stand.
My principles are guarded with utmost pride and dignity - MY!
I walk and live a virtuous life knowing that GOD will send the
one for me.
Children are priority - Is this a surprise, certain things because
of them we should not compromise.
I cannot help who I am for it is the CREATOR who created
my purity.
From this experience I have gained.
My glory, My glory, My glory.
My glory, pride and dignity will remain the same.

Glory I AM

Glory I AM, and for years I extended this to you. One day I awoke and it seemed as if in a days time the glory I extended to you, you let it go.

What seemed as if, became a reality.

years ago, I prayed that the right one for me would arrive. At you I looked feeling of course you were the one.

As I place my mind on the future, I have ceased to wonder why across my path you fly.

From here where do I go. Our children will always be priority, this is not a surprise, certain things because of them we will not compromise.

As I receive directions from the All-in-All., I know for sure I have ceased to wonder why.

While on my path from this day on, my thoughts are no longer of you.

Glory I AM, and for years I extended this to you. In a days time you let it go.

My principles remain guarded. My pride and dignity. Glory I AM they were regained,

IN FACT AS SOON AS YOU LEFT OUT OF THE DOOR.

All For A Religious Plea

The THREE of Us Are Here...
Daddy where are you.
We Miss The Things We Used to DO and how we used to BE.
We miss hearing you say when the times get rough the tough get going.
These words created a strength in us that mommy and you instilled.
Why Did You Leave.
We are sure when you begin to see out of the darkness you will be.

Our needs, though mommy is hard at work, its hard for them to be met.
Daddy it took both mommy and you to give all that we were to get.
Why did you leave us Three all for a religious plea.
   KASSINDA, KAMEELAH, DENNIS II
   DADDY, WE LOVE AND MISS YOU!

On Relationships

The Male Ego.
The Males Need To Share.
The Male Spirituality, who could give a care.
The Male and Female
The Female Ego
The Females need to be possessive and monogomous
The Females need not to share a male.
The Female Spirituality. Oh! how homogeneous.
The Female and Male

Cassandra Huff

...AND THERE HE STOOD LOOKING AT ME...

HIS SMILE WAS SINCERE,
HIS VIBRATIONS WERE GENTLE,
HIS REPOSE WAS CALM AND PEACEFUL,
FOREVER I WOULD WANT US TO BE...

bEGGIN PLEASE

dO YOU WANT ME TO GET ON MY KNEES AND BEG
    pLEASE
IT'S NOT GOING TO HAPPEN
I'M STRONG, WITH BOTH OUTER AND INNER STRENGTH
    SMART AND PRETTY, UH! HU!
SO GET IN MY FACE IF YOU WANT TO DON'T COME TALKIN TO ME ABOUT
    BEGGIN PLEASE
    I WILL JUST SNAP SO FAST CAUSE I AIN'T BEGGIN...PLEASE.

KAMEELAH DENSUA JAHI WILLIAMS

BUTTERFLY

COURAGE TO CHANGE

WHO BEGAN ALL WRAPPED UP AS IN
A COCOON, THROUGH METAMORPHOSIS
EMERGED THEN AS A CATERPILLAR
INTO A 'BEAUTIFUL BUTTERFLY'.

SO SHALL YOU THROUGH
METAMORPHOSIS EVOLVE INTO A NEW
BEING, METAPHORICALLY SO...

YOUR NEW WINGS SHALL TAKE YOU
TO PLACES SO HIGH...
A NEW BEGINNING.
  A NEW TOMORROW.
    A NEW YOU...

SO FILLED WITH <u>JOY</u> ONLY **YOU** WILL UNDERSTAND...
The
"TransformatioN"

KURCHUMBE

LIKE LIGHTENING FLASH
UNGHI   -   KEAH   -   COMBAT ZONE
Got to be a leader... Let the leader lead
Chamber - Strike- Block
Visualize - Materialize
Like Lightening Flash

Kucha - Karate'

I AM HOLY SO IS HE

FOR I AM HOLY...AT HIM I LOOK FEELING HE TOO IS HOLY.
MY SPIRIT WAS CHECKED SO INDEED I KNOW THAT HE IS HOLY.

As I take my mind off of this predominate thought I place it (my mind)
on what I would like the future to hold. GOD is my guide... For it is GOD
that holds the future, and therefore GOD is my ARMOR.

So From Here Where Do We Go:

My principles are guarded
...My pride and dignity are my armor.
   My integrity allows me to remain in tact.

My prayers maintain my self control

My virtuousness allows me to feel that spiritual warmth that
illuminates from him.

The joyfulness of becoming enlightened on a higher level exudes from his
vibrations, and only quickens my desire to be... that that GOD has created
in pairs, male and female... His companion.

The CREATOR has created my purity...and has revealed the restoration of his,
FOR HE WALKS A RIGHTEOUS WALK, and the reality is shown for his
armor is his sincerity.

BLOOMS

Like a flower
　　She Grows
Like a flower
　　She Flourishes
Absorbing The Good of The ALL

　　Sharing What Has Been Bestowed
　　　　She Graces The Wholeness...

THE CREATOR OF US ALL -
　　　　　　BLOOMS

I Need A Pet

Mommy it's just not fair
You have me, kassinda, and kameelah
I don't have anyone, I need a cat and dog to love
and care for
You do that for us
My heart is broken I need a pet.
Auntie Vennie has dogs
Papa has a dog
I need a pet so my heart won't be broken.

Moral: Everyone wants to be loved and cared for, everyone wants to share
   love and care. Everyone.

12/1/95 A 5 year olds concept of loving and caring.

Dennis Williams II

BUT AM I NOT

I wish I was clean as the air I breath,
But AM I NOT
As pure as the water I drink,
But AM I NOT
As plentiful as the dirt in the street,
But AM I NOT
I am a young girl.
Not knowing my future, but thinking of
my past I forge ahead,
Not knowing what it will bring forth
But cherishing what it has brung forth.
MY SPIRIT IS PURE.
I forge ahead.
CHERISHING ALL THAT IS.

Kassinda Densua Joi' Williams

SELF

I think of my self as an enlightenment to my own life and
as well to others.
My goals are to finish high school with a 4.0 or better. I
plan to go to Georgia Tech, MIT, Tuskegee, or Clemson.
I think it is important for everyone to have goals. Every
school year I write a list of things I want to accomplish.
Goals are kind of a path of learning, because each time you
reach a goal you know more than you did before.
For as long as I can remember, I've wanted to be a teacher, a
lawyer, and an engineer. If there was a job that combined all three
at once I would do it. Since the new age is technology, engineering
is the best bet. If that doesn't work out I can be a teacher, or
follow in the footsteps of my mom, with hopes of going to law school
sometime in her 40's.
Whatever my goals are I want to reach them and finish top of the class.
My mom is an inspiration to me. In many ways she's strong,
independent and gives so much to everyone else. The only time
she has for her self is in the car going to work. My mom has
degrees and is still going to school. If the world gave out awards
for caring, understanding, loving, strong willed women, my mom
would be first on their list.
When I listen to all this talk about prayer in school it makes me
think are we doing what's best for the children or what's best for
the parents. I have many pros and cons about this issue. My pros
are the student gets in touch with his/her inner self. My cons are
I don't think the children are speaking out enough. Personally I
think it's wrong to dictate to anyone what religion they should
follow. Any way if they had prayer in school they would have to
create a school for each religion, each denomination. There would
be more schools than there are homes. My views on many things
are mixed because there are always pros and cons.
Soccer is a great sport. I've been playing for quiet a few years.
I was delighted when I made Athena. I think soccer is a way out of
pressure for me. When I get to practice or a game I see new faces
other than the ones I see at home and school.
Computers fascinate me that's why I have one of my own. I at
least try to work with each day.
Me as a person I think I'm smart and have a lot going for me.
The only thing time can do for me is to make me better.

Kassinda Densua Joi' Williams

...CAN WE...

GO JOGGING
  SKATING
    SWIMMING
      BICYCLING
        PLAY TENNIS

TO THE MOVIES... ON A PICNIC
  TAKE A PITCURE
    GO TO SAPLO ISLAND
      TO THE BEACH...BAREFOOTED IN THE SAND
        JAMAICA HILTON
          HEAD
            FORREST HILLS
              SUN DIAL
                BAHAMAS OR HAWAII

CAN YOU GO LOOK AT CARS WITH ME... LOOK AT A PLAY...
  CAN WE GO TO THE LIBRARY,
    MEETINGS...

CAN YOU MEET MY CHILDREN AND BE A POSITIVE ROLE MODEL.

YOU WANT SOMEBODY TO PLAY WITH... GO GET YOU A TOY.

CAN YOU CALL ME DURING THE WEEK AT YOUR CONVENIENCE.
  FOOTBALL GAMES...SOCCER...SWIM MEETS...
  BASKETBALL/BASEBALL GAMES, OH BOY!

STAY OVERNIGHT, YOU CAN'T COME TO MY HOUSE.
EVERYOTHER WEEKEND CAN WE RENT A CABIN OR SUITE.

CAN WE GO OUT TO DINNER... CAN WE... SHARE TALL CAKE
AT RUBY TUESDAY!
CAN WE MAKE LOVE WITHOUT FEELING GUILTY...SECRET LOVERS?
  YOU HAVE A SPOUSE I DON'T.
  WHAT ABOUT FLOWERS CAN YOU SHOWER ME WITH THEM
  OCCASSIONALLY, AND JEWELRY TOO, LET'S TALK ABOUT
THAT... A NICE OUTFIT OR TWO.

WHEN I REALLY NEED YOU BE THERE FOR ME, I'LL BE THERE FOR
YOU!...
CAN YOU GIVE ME AN EMBRACE, OR A SMACK ON THE LIPS...
WHENEVER YOU WANT TO.
CAN YOU TAKE CARE OF ME AS WELL AS YOU TAKE CARE OF
HOME!!

CAN WE... CAN WE DO THESE THINGS TOGETHER...**WE CAN**?
...CAN WE...

Cassandra Huff

THE STAR OF ALL STARS

tHE STAR OF ALL sTARS
            IS YET TO BE SEEN,
       THE STAR OF ALL STARS IS IN
         THE EYES OF WHO BELIEVES.
kASSINDA dENSUA jOI' wILLIAMS

THE CRACKS OF LIFE

THE CRACKS OF LIFE WHICH EVERYONE FALLS THROUGH
ONE TIME OR ANOTHER.
MAYBE THE STARS ARE TO HELP SOME GO UPWARD. LOOK TOWARDS
THE STARS.
THE CRACKS OF LIFE YOU WILL THEN AVOID FALLING THROUGH.

kASSINDA DENSUE JOI' WILLIAMS

PEACE

You put something on my mind...PEACE.
What is this something that you have put
on my mind...PEACE
You put something on my mind...PEACE.

A Friend...My Friend

A Friend...My Friend
I can be... You can Be...
Who and what we are
To Be...
And still be
A FRIEND...MY FRIEND...

THIS WOMAN OF DIGNITY

TELL ME WHO IS THIS WOMAN OF DIGNITY.
THIS WOMAN OF SUBSTANCE...OF TRUTH.
THIS WOMAN OF DIGNIFIED GRACE...
OF STRENGTH.

FOR I HAVE SPOKEN - ONLY TRUTH...
DIRECTION AND GUIDANCE FROM THE ALL-IN-ALL
I MUST STANDFAST, FOR WHAT PROCEEDETH
FROM THIS VESSEL IS ONLY THE TRUTH OF
THE LIVING OMNIPRESENCE.

SPEAK OF FREEDOM FOR IT IS WRITTEN
"THE LORD IS THAT SPIRIT AND WHERE
THE SPIRIT OF THE LORD IS THERE IS LIBERTY"

TELL ME WHO IS THIS WOMAN OF LIBERTY.
THIS WOMAN WHO RECEIVES FROM THE
POWERHOUSE OF THE ALL-IN-ALL...
CULTIVATED WITH DIGNIFIED GRACE.

TELL ME WHO IS THIS WOMAN...
HER FAITH SHALL CONTINUE TO BE...
BE NOT CONFUSED...
BE NOT SWAYED...
FOR THIS WOMAN IS FREE, THIS WOMAN OF DIGNITY, OF LIBERTY.

Tom Wilson

teamwork
trap
pass
go wide
control
play your positions
push up
heel to toe
what are you doing
pay attention
go lady "attack"

Kassinda D.J. Williams "mommy I want to remember coach Wilson as I saw him last, watching a soccer game in the ready position, one foot before the other, as if ready to run out on the field to rescue one of his girls, "LADY ATTACK"

Cassandra Huff

DISTINGUISHED CLOSENESS

I HAVE A NEED TO EXPERIENCE DISTINGQUISHED CLOSENESS
THE MIND AND ENERGY ACTIVATED IS THE BEING STAGE
I HAVE A NEED FOR SOMEONE TO OFFER ME
A MUTUAL RELATIONSHIP, AS OPPOSED TO JUST BEING
MARRIED,
I NEED TO BE WITH MY IDEAL, SOMEONE WHO
WANTS TO BE WITH ME.
I HAVE A NEED FOR DISTINGUISHED CLOSENESS
A COMPLIMENT, A COMPANION, A
CLEAR COMMITTMENT TO ME.

mAKING aMENDS

YOU CAN'T SAY YOUR SORRY BUT I KNOW YOU ARE
WE RECOGNIZE THAT ONLY LOVE IS REAL AND
EVERYTHING ELSE IS FEAR.

FORGIVENESS BECOMES A PROCESS, AND SOME KIND
OF WAY SOMETIMES WE MISS THE MARK AND CREATE
UNHEALED PLACES THAT SEEMED TO BE FAULTS

WHEN THE EGO TAKES CONTROL, WE MAKE ERRORS
REALLY WE ARE NOT THE ERRORS

WE HAVE BEEN SEVERED BUT WE ARE BACK TOGETHER
WE HAVE COME BACK TOGETHER WITH A STRONGER
HEAVIER BOND.

THE ULTIMATE REALITY IS A MYSTERY

BEING HUMAN SURELY YOU HAVE FEELINGS.. AND FEEL ANGER...
BEING VINDICTIVE IS NOT THE CURE...
THOSE THAT ARE VINDICTIVE ARE THOSE OF DECEIFUL SPIRIT
SUFFERING OPEN AMBUSH GIVES ADDITIONAL STRENGTH;
AND FORTITUDE
IT MAKES YOU UNDERSTAND THAT "EACH WALKS THIS
WALK ALONE",
FOR IT IS OUR FELLOW BEINGS THAT HAVE YET TO
ASPIRE TO THE DEPTHS OF "REALITY"
EACH TIME WE WALK THIS PLANET EARTH OUR
LEVEL OF CONSCIOUSNESS INCREASES.
CAN WE SPEAK TO OUR BEFORE COMINGS - AMONGST
US ARE THOSE OF LOWER LEVELS OF CONSCIOUSNESS.
THESE BEINGS ARE NOT TO BE CHALLANGED.
MY EXPERIENCES BRING OUT THE BEST IN ME,
THE ULTIMATE REALITY IS A MYSTERY.

THE GARNET GEM

TRUTH AND FRIENDSHIP IS WHAT THIS GEM REPRESENTS
IN ALIGNMENT IT MUST BE. WHATEVER IT MEANS
TO YOU DOES NOT MATTER, FOR I KNOW WHAT
IT MEANS TO ME.

THE GEM GARNET THAT I KNOW IS AN ORIGINALITY,
THIS IS A REALITY THAT WILL ALWAYS
BE A PART OF ME.

THOUGH ITS TRUTH AND FRIENDSHIP IS SHEER
ITS INNER DIMENSION
IS HARD TO PEER, FOR THERE IS NO
MATCH OR EQUAL, FAR OR NEAR

IT MAY BE HARD TO FIND AGAIN AS ITS GOODNESS IS FROM GOD...
SO ONCE ATTACHED TO THIS GEM NEVER LET IT GO.

THE GEM GARNET IS A GEM THAT REPRESENTS MUCH MORE
THAN ANYONE WOULD EVER KNOW...

IT IS KNOWN FOR ITS LOVE AND COMPASSION,
AS IT STRENGTHENS AND PURIFIES.
THE GEM GARNET I CAN TELL YOU, KNOWS HOW TO CREATE HARMONY.
FOR THE TRUTH IT REPRESENTS
IS OFTEN UNEASILY FOUND, THIS IS ONE
GEM YOU WILL ALWAYS
WANT AROUND
IN ITS DEEPEST TRANSPARENT RED, IT IS
A MOST PRECIOUS MINERAL OF VARIOUS COLORS AND HUE,
AND I WILL TELL YOU ONE THING THIS GEM GARNET
IS HARD TO SEE THROUGH.
IN HONESTY IT REVEALS THE TRUTH OF WHAT YOU DO NEED TO KNOW
AND THIS GEM GARNET IS TRUE, IN ALL SINCERITY.

IT WOULD BE HARD TO DETACH FROM THIS GEM, IT WOULD BE HARD
TO LET IT GO FOR WHAT IT REPRESENTS IS ETERNAL TRUTH ... I KNOW.
ONCE IT GRASPS YOUR HEART
YOU TRULY WILL NOT EVER WANT IT TO DEPART.
MIND YOU...THE TRUTH IT REPRESENTS IS GENUINE.

OF GOD

I SEEK THE ULTIMATE PERFECTION... WONDERING FROM WHERE HAVE I COME.
MY SOULS EXPERIENCES ARE MANY; I WONDER WHAT PURPOSE THIS TIME HAS MY SOUL.
THE STRUGGLES ARE SIMILAR TO THE STRUGGLES BEFORE. I WONDER WHAT ACTS AM I REPEATING... AM I REAPING WHAT I SOWED?

SO MUCH GOES UNTOLD BECAUSE I KNOW NOT FROM WHERE I COME.
FROM LIFE TO LIFE I GO AS MY SOUL SEEKS TO KNOW THE ULTIMATE PERFECTION.

THE ESSENCE OF ME IS MY HEART AND SOUL, AND THESE ARE OF GOD, SO I AM TOLD.

I HAD A DOLL NOT A RAG DOLL

WHEN I WAS A LITTLE GIRL I HAD A RAG DOLL...

NO, NO, NO
IT WASN'T WHEN I WAS A LITTLE GIRL I HAD A RAG DOLL... I HAD
A DOLL, WHEN I WAS A LITTLE GIRL.
I DIDN'T KNOW MY DOLL WAS A RAG DOLL...
NO, NO, NO

MY DOLL WAS A REAL DOLL, A PRETTY DOLL, A GOOD DOLL...
SOMETIMES A BAD DOLL...
MY DOLL WAS MY DOLL...
NOT A <u>RAG</u> DOLL...
WHEN I WAS A LITTLE GIRL
I HAD A DOLL... THAT DOLL AS PRETTY AS IT COULD BE,
PLAYED WITH ME...
TALKED WITH ME...
ATE WITH ME...
MOTIVATED ME...
ENCOURAGED ME...
PRAYED WITH ME...
SOMETIMES THAT DOLL WAS MY BROTHER, MOTHER, FATHER, SISTER,
AUNT, CHILD, COUSIN, FRIEND, GRANDMOTHER, GRANDFATHER...
A TOY FROM THE STORE...
SOME STICKS I PUT TOGETHER FROM OUT THE YARD.

THAT WAS MY DOLL.

I HAD A DOLL, NOT A <u>RAG</u> DOLL.

Roller Coaster

life is like a roller coaster
up and down
swaying to the side
up and down and around
swoosh, feel that breeze, it is few and far between.
where are you going on this here roller coaster
this life is like a roller coaster "ride".

NEW BIRTH AWAKENING

THE WINTER SOLISTICE ARE THE DAYS OF LIGHT
AFTER WHICH THERE IS AN AWAKENING
THE NEWNESS OF WHO WE ARE BRING SOLICE TO
OUR BEING.

WE ARE THE CLAY

"WE ARE THE CLAY AND THOU ART OUR POTTER, AND WE ALL
ARE THE WORK OF THY HAND".

EVERYTHING THAT HAPPENS, HAPPENS BECAUSE THE ULTIMATE
POWER - THE GOD - ALLOWS IT TO HAPPEN...
IT COULD NOT OTHERWISE BE.
GOD TOOK US AND FORMED US INTO WHO HE WANTED US TO BE
AND NOW WE MUST REALIZE OUR ESSENCE AS THE
MASTER BLUE PRINT HAS IT.

A SHATTERED FEELING

ONE DAY MY MOM SAT ME, MY SISTER, AND MY BROTHER DOWN
AND SAID THIS MOMENT I MUST TELL YOU THREE
   YOUR DAD AND I ARE MOVING ON TOGETHER WE WILL NOT LIVE
    FROM THIS DAY AS ONE.
        AFTER HEARING THESE WORDS THAT SHATTERED MY FEELINGS
        SHED TEARS DID I, I CRIED, BUT I KNOW BECAUSE OF WHO
    MY MOM IS I WILL BE LIVING ON.

        I AM WITHOUT MY DAD. MY SISTER, BROTHER, AND MOM
            I STILL HAVE. I WILL NOT CRY NO MORE. I DID GET THROUGH
                THIS SHATTERED FEELING
            MY DAD I WILL CONTINUE TO LOVE DAY BY DAY.
            I WILL ALWAYS LOVE MY MOM, BECAUSE I
            UNDERSTAND AND KNOW HER WAY.

                    KAMEELAH DENSUA JAHI WILLIAMS

THE UNTHINKABLE

THE IDEA OF YOU WANDERING INTO
THE ABSOLUTE ETERNITY IS ALMOST
THE UNTHINKABLE.

KASSINDA DENSUA JOI' WILLIAMS

MY BEGINNING

I WONDER IS THIS JUST ME OR THE BEGINNING OF THE
END... THE END IS FOR ALL THOSE WHO ARE LOST.
THEREFORE THIS IS MY BEGINNING AND I
CHOOSE NOT TO MEET MY ENDING.

KASSINDA DENSUA JOI' WILLIAMS

Cassandra Huff

THE DAY I FALL IN LOVE

THE DAY I FALL IN LOVE, IS THE DAY I FALL IN LOVE.
AS FAR AS I CAN TELL LOVE HAS SO MANY PHASES,
I MIGHT FALL IN LOVE IN DIFFERENT GROWTH STAGES.

KASSINDA DENSUA JOI' WILLIAMS

LIGHTENING MY MOMS LOAD

I *KASSINDA DENSUA JOI' WILLIAMS*, TO LIGHTEN MY MOMS LOAD,
TAKE ON THE FOLLOWING RESPONSIBILITIES AS A 15 YEAR OLD.
BY WASHING THE DISHES (THIS INCLUDES THE TABLE AND
STOVE) EVERY OTHER DAY STARTING WITH TODAY. I ALSO
WILL WASH AND FOLD THE CLOTHES PRESENTLY IN THE LAUNDRY
ROOM, AFTER THIS HAS BEEN COMPLETED I WILL THEREON
WASH AND FOLD CLOTHES EVERY DAY OPPOSITE THE DISHES I
WASH. I ALSO WILL KEEP MY ROOM CLEAN IN A DECENT FASHION,
THIS IS INCLUDING THE UPSTAIRS BATHROOM. BUT IF
I SEE KAMEELAH OR DENNIS MAKING A DELIBERATE MESS, I
WILL REPORT THE SITUATION TO YOU, I HOPE THIS IS IN KEEPING
WITH WHAT YOU WOULD LIKE FOR ME TO DO AT THE RESIDENCE.
I AM TRYING TO LIGHTEN YOUR LOAD MOM, SO YOUR MIND AT WORK
CAN REST.

KASSINDA DENSUA JOI' WILLIAMS

Cassandra Huff

PAIN

WHAT IS THIS THAT WE CALL PAIN
CAN SOMEONE TELL ME, CAN SOMEONE DESCRIBE
THIS UNEASINESS, THIS PAIN.

IS PAIN A FEELING, I OFTEN QUESTION, OR IS IT JUST AN
EMOTION SELF CREATED.
HOW DO I MAKE THIS PAIN GO AWAY, AS I QUESTION
WHY IT IS THIS WAY.

THE HOLIEST ACT

THE HOLIEST ACT I AM TOLD IS THE ACTS OF ALL ACTS.
YOU KNOW THE SEX ACT.
THESE MOMENTS OF INTERCOURSE YOU SEE
ARE SPIRITUAL AND DIVINELY.
THE CREATOR CREATED US, A COMPANION, A MATE
IT IS OUR DIVINE RIGHT, TO SHARE THIS HOLIEST
ACT... WITH A COMMITTED COMPANION, A MATE
THE SACREDNESS OF WHAT WE SHARE.

IT IS THROUGH THIS HOLIEST ACT WE RECEIVE A CONFIRMATION
OF OUR REALITY.

FOR IT IS THROUGH THIS HOLY UNION OUR SOULS PERFECT UNITY IS
ATTAINED. AND WHEN WE UNIFY IN THIS HOLIEST ACT OUR
TRUE BLESSINGS WE CLEARLY SEE.

VICTIMS STATEMENT

TO KNOW <u>YOU</u> RIGHT... SOMETIMES IS NOT ENOUGH...
I REMAINED HUMANE... IT SEEMED AS IF I FOUGHT ALONE.
    THOUGH OTHERS FOUGHT A SILENT FIGHT... TO ASSURE
            ALONE I WOULD NOT BE.
I REMAIN HUMANE... IN THE STATE OF UNFAIRNESS THAT DOES EXIST...
    AN ALWAYS HAVE, PERHAPS EVEN ALWAYS WILL...
SUFFERING, REGARDLESS... JUST BEING HUMANE.
                SANCTIONS:
                REPRIMAND
                DISBARMENT
                ADMONITION
                PROBATION
                SUSPENSION
THE INTERWORKINGS OF THE MIND... NO ONE REALLY KNOWS... BUT
        THAT DOES NOT SAY THE UNPRESENTABLE PAIN AND SUFFERING
        IT UNDERGOES.
                STRIVE TO OVERCOME HARDWORK AND THE STINCH OF
                POVERTY... OH HOW MANY HAVE EXPERIENCED THIS.
                AVOIDED MENIAL TASKS AND POVERTY BECAUSE OF THE
                HARDWORK AND IMPOVERISHED CONDITIONS OF PARENTS
                AND FOREPARENTS... OH THE CONDITIONS THEY ENDURED
                IN HOPES THAT THEIR SEED WOULD RISE ABOVE.
FROM WHENCE WE CAME, AND WHERE WE GO...OUR DESTINY ONLY
        HE CAN SEE!!!!!
KINGS REMAIN KINGS
QUEENS REMAIN QUEENS
PAWNS, PAWNS
SERVANTS, SERVANTS
CHIEFS, CHIEFS
SLAVES, SLAVES
SLAVEMASTERS, SLAVEMASTERS
    ...WHETHER FREED OR NOT...
        I MY PEOPLE AM THE PROGENY OF KINGS, QUEENS, CHIEFS, AND
        SLAVEMASTERS... THEREFORE A QUEEN.

WHAT RACE HAS TO DO WITH JUSTICE IS UNBEKNOWNST TO ME
...THE MISTREATMENT OF PEOPLE - COLOR IT DOES NOT SEE...
            I REMAIN HUMANE

IS THE TRUTH REALLY HEARD

THE QUESTION BECOMES IS THE TRUTH REALLY HEARD... OFTEN...
WHEN IT SHOULD BE.
WE LIVE IN A SOCIETY WHERE IT IS HARD TO GET FREE REPRESENTATION,
AND EVEN IF YOU PAY, "NO BODY HAS TIME"
OVER AND OVER AGAIN THE DOLLAR BILL IS USED TO
MISTREAT PEOPLE CAN'T YOU SEE.
WE LIVE IN A SOCIETY WHERE SOME WOMEN AND MEN "SWORN IN"
STILL LIE...
THE JUSTICE CENTER AND LEGAL AID...
"THESE CASES ARE SCREENED"
ALL CASES, WITHOUT APPROPRIATE LEGAL REPRESENTATION, A
COURT APPOINTED ATTORNEY, SHOULD BE...
PRO SE REPRESENTATION SHOULD BE ABOLISHED FOR IT
IS IN THIS STAGE THE TRUTH IS MOSTLY NOT ALLOWED
TO BE HEARD.
WE LIVE IN A SOCIETY WHERE SUFFICIENT UNTO TODAY IS THE EVIL
THEREOF, AND WHERE EVERY EVIL IS NOT PUNISHED, AND EVERY
GOOD DEED NOT REWARDED.
WHERE FACTS ARE NOT FACTS, AND SOMETIMES EVIDENTIARY
TRUTHS DON'T MATTER.
IT WAS RULED THAT WHAT WAS SUBMITTED WOULD BE
REVIEWED AND THAT I REMAINED PROTECTED THANKFUL ME!
IN ALL MY PAIN AND SUFFERING THROUGHOUT THIS EXPERIENCE...
AND OH! HOW I HAVE SUFFERED... IN THE WORDS OF
JESS STEARN "EVERY KNEE SHALL BOW" WHERE IS THE
JUSTICE, YOUR HONOR, JUDICIALLY.
I WILL GET NO MONETARY SATISFACTION FOR THIS UNDUE
HARDSHIP. WHO KNOWS MY DESTINY AND HOW THIS
HARDSHIP WILL EFFECT ME! MENTALLY, EMOTIONALLY,
OR PHYSICALLY!
HOWEVER, MY PROPERTY I AM TO HAVE AND MY CHILDREN
REMAIN PLACED AND ROOTED.
FOR THIS AM I TO BE GRATEFUL,
AM I TO BE THANKFUL,
ONLY THE JUDGE IS TO DECIDE.

LET THE JUDGE DECIDE

THINGS CHANGE

YOU TELL ME THINGS CHANGE
FOR BETTER FOR WORSE
STAGNANT, PROGRESSIVE THINGS DO CHANGE.
CAN WE IDENTIFY THESE THINGS THAT CHANGE
AT WHAT POINT DO THINGS CHANGE TO BRING
INTO FRUITION THE TRUE EXISTENCE OF
WHAT SHOULD BE..
I AM TOLD THAT CHANGE IS ENVITABLE
IS THIS TO SAY A CONSTANT STATE
OF CHANGE IS OUR HISTORY.
SOME THINGS I DESIRE NOT TO CHANGE
ESPECIALLY MY FEELINGS OF ECSTASY I HAVE
FOR YOU.

MY BEAUTIFUL BLACK SISTERS STANDING TALL

ALL SHADES
ALBINO TO CHARCOAL
ANCESTRAL CHARACTERISTICS...
PERSONALITIES PAST AND PRESENT...
DRESSED IN VARIOUS ETHNIC STYLES...EUROPEAN, ARABIC, AFRICAN, AMERICAN.
SILK...POLYSTER...RAYON...SHEER...SYNTHETICS!
MY BEAUTIFUL BLACK SISTERS STANDING TALL!
SOME LOST...SOME SEARCHING...SEEKING...SOME SAVED...FOUND.
WHAT'S GOING THROUGH OUR MINDS...
SOME PROPER...SOME CULTURED...SOME NOT...MY BEAUTIFUL BLACK
SISTERS, WHO ARE WE...WHO DO YOU LOVE...ALL STANDING SO TALL
WHO DO YOU KNOW...WHO DO YOU REPRESENT.
WHAT IS YOUR LIFE'S DESTINY...RESPECT.., LIFE'S ESSENTIAL TOOL.
SOME GODLY...SOME NOT!
ARE WE LOVED... ARE WE PROTECTED... ARE WE REALLY EVER GOING TO BE
LOVED AND RESPECTED...
MY BEAUTIFUL BLACK SISTERS STANDING TALL...
IS THERE TRUE UNITY AMONGST US.. IS THERE.
DO WE LOVE AND RESPECT OURSELVES, THEREFORE US.
MY BEAUTIFUL BLACK SISTERS STANDING TALL... IN ALL THESE SHADES...
ALBINO TO CHARCOAL.
DO WE KNOW OUR BEGINNINGS, WHO WE ARE, DO WE KNOW OUR DESTINY.
STRAIGHT HAIR, CORN ROLLS, DREADLOCKS, SHORT HAIR, LONG HAIR, TWISTS,
CURLS, BRAIDS, NATURALS, WAVES, KINKS, GARBS, SCARVES, KUFI'S,
TURBANS, HEAD BANDS, HEAD WRAPS, RIBBONS IN OUR HAIR...
DO WE KNOW WHO WE ARE.
EARRINGS IN OUR EARS (LOTS OF THEM) 1, 2, 3, 4 & 5...
EARRINGS IN OUR NOSE, BRACLETS ON OUR ARMS, ANKLES, NECKLACES -
CHARMS OF ALL SORTS.
ADORN YOURSELVES, MY SISTERS, MY BEAUTIFUL BLACK SISTERS STANDING
TALL... WHO ARE WE DO WE KNOW WHO WE ARE...
JEWELS, STONES OF ALL SORTS, DIAMONDS, RUBIES, SIMULATED - REAL,
SAPPHIRES, EMERALDS, JADES, STERLING, BRASS, ZIRCONIC, PEWTER.

Cassandra Huff

MY BEAUTIFUL BLACK SISTERS STANDING TALL
"The Essence of Black Beauty Strength"

SHOES, HIGH TOPS, LOW TOPS, SANDLES, SLIDES, PUMPS, SNEAKERS, LEATHER, PATENT LEATHER, CLOTH, SUEDE... DO WE KNOW WHO WE ARE...

SINGLE, MARRIED, DIVORCED, SEPARATED, WITH CHILD, WITHOUT CHILD... DO WE KNOW WHO WE ARE...
    SOME STRONG, SOME WEAK, SOME WITH FOUNDATION, SOME WITHOUT...

LITERATE, ILLITERATE, LEARNED, UNLEARNED, EDUCATED, UNEDUCATED, GIFTED, UNGIFTED, INTELLIGENT, INTELLECTUAL, DIVINE... MY BEAUTIFUL BLACK SISTERS STANDING TALL... DO WE KNOW WHO WE ARE...

MY BEAUTIFUL BLACK SISTERS STANDING TALL.. WHO ARE WE!

    BABIES IN OUR ARMS, GRANDMOTHERS, MOTHERS, AUNTS, DAUGHTERS, NEICES BY OUR SIDES.

INNER BEAUTY... OUTER, DO WE KNOW WHO WE ARE!

MY BEAUTIFUL BLACK SISTERS HOW DIVIDED WE {SOME OF US!} STAND... STANDING TALL!!

WHERE IS THE BLACKMAN

I'LL TELL YOU WHERE THE BLACKMAN IS:

TAKING CARE OF BUSINESS UNDER THE COVERS - THAT'S WHERE HE IS.

NOT ALL OF THEM BUT MOST OF THEM ARE RUNNING FROM PILLAR TO POST TRYING TO SEE HOW MANY BABIES THEY CAN MAKE, TO PROVE THAT THEY ARE A MAN... IS THIS REALLY A MAN... WHERE IS THE BLACKMAN.

RUNNING FROM PILLAR TO POST TRYING TO SEE HOW MANY WIVES HE CAN GET AT THE SAME TIME... TO PROVE HIS MANHOOD... IS THIS REALLY A MAN.
WHERE IS THE BLACKMAN.
I'LL TELL YOU WHERE THE BLACKMAN IS:
WHERE IS THE BLACK MAN... TRYING TO GET ALL HIS WIVES TO SEE THAT EACH OF THEM MUST WAIT HER TURN TO BE WITH HIM EVEN THOUGH IT'S A STRUGGLE TO TAKE CARE OF THE NEEDS OF ONE WIFE HE STILL WANTS MANY WIVES.

OH BLACKMAN WHERE ARE YOU... WE NEED YOU... WE ARE WAITING FOR YOU.

WHERE IS THE BLACKMAN. WE NEED HIM. THE REAL BLACK MAN. HE ONCE WAS A KING.. HE ONCE WAS GREAT... BUT NOW HE'S FALLEN.

GREAT BLACKMAN WHERE ARE YOU... WHAT HAVE YOU BECOME... WHO ARE YOU...

WHERE IS HE...AT HOME IN BED WITH HIS CO-WIFE...

I FOUND HIM, I FOUND HIM... THE BLACKMAN, AND WHEN I FOUND HIM I ASKED HIM WHAT WAS IMPORTANT TO HIM?... AND HE SAID: HOW MANY WIVES I CAN HAVE AND HOW MANY BABIES I CAN MAKE.

IS HE WORKING PROVIDING FOR HIS FAMILY.
IS HE IN THE FIELD TILLING THE LAND... BUYING LAND
OH BLACKMAN, ARE YOU CONSTRUCTING A BUILDING, RENOVATING YOUR HOME, DID YOU TURN IN PAYROLL TODAY... TURN IN THE BID. ARE YOU PARTICIPATING IN YOUR CHILDRENS ACTIVITIES - TEACHING THEM, YOUR CHILDREN, ARE YOU TEACHING THEM OR SOMEONE ELSES, OH BLACKMAN.

WHERE IS THE BLACKMAN

WHERE IS HE...AT HOME IN BED WITH HIS CO-WIFE...
I CAN'T FIND HIM. WHO DO YOU DEFEND... CAN YOU DEFEND ME?
    BLACKMAN WHERE ARE YOU.

WHERE IS HE... TRYING TO SEE HOW MANY WIVES HE CAN GET.

OWNING YOUR OWN BUILDING, DOING SOMETHING FOR YOURSELF...

IS HE TENDING TO THE RENTAL PROPERTY OR JUST LETTING IT GO.
ALL THIS DEBT ARE THE CO-WIVES GOING TO HELP PAY IT, YOU KNOW
ALL THIS DEBT - WE'RE SUPPOSED TO BE A BIG FAMILY... LET'S ALL
SHARE IN ON THESE RESPONSIBITIES. ISN'T THAT WHAT FAMILIES DO!

COME ON BLACKMAN... WHERE IS THE REAL BLACKMAN...

BLACKMAN WHERE - JUST WHERE ARE YOU, BLACKMAN.

ISN'T ALL THIS SUPPOSED TO ENHANCE EVERYONE INVOLVED...
BLACKMAN BE FOR REAL.

WHERE IS HE... SOMEWHERE IN BED MAKING ... YOU SAY, YOU CALL THAT LOVE.

JUMPING FROM PILLAR TO POST.

HOW MANY PEOPLE DO YOU EMPLOY WHERE IS YOUR BUSINESS...

ARE YOU DOING COMMUNITY WORK... WORK FOR GOD... WHAT KIND OF
WORK ARE YOU DOING FOR YOUR FELLOWMAN.

WHERE IS THE BLACKMAN... THE REAL BLACKMAN...

         PRESIDENT WHERE IS THE BLACKMAN... THE ONE THAT APPRECIATES
         ME FOR WHO I AM, AND HAS ENOUGH DIGNITY TO NOT
         WANT TO SHAM.

PUT ON THE VEIL, COVER MY HEAD, COVER MY BODY FROM HEAD TO TOE,
BLACKMAN PLEASE YOU BETTER LEARN HOW TO CONTAIN YOURSELF
RUNNING FROM PILLAR TO POST, FROM ONE WIFE TO - TO - TO -
HOW MANY DO YOU WANT - TWO - YOU SURE YOU DON'T WANT FOUR
(1, 2, 3, 4) SAY SPEND 4 HOURS HERE AND FOUR HOURS THERE-
BLACKMAN PLEASE, THAT'S HOW MANY CHILDREN YOU HAVE,
IS THIS MANHOOD.

WHERE IS THE BLACKMAN

WHERE IS THE BLACK MAN... THE REAL BLACKMAN... THIS HAS NOTHING TO
DO WITH FORGIVING THIS HAS TO DO WITH WHERE YOU ARE - AND WHO
YOU WANT TO BE - THIS HAS NOTHING TO DO WITH WHO YOUR GOD IS OR
WHAT NATIONALITY YOU ARE - THIS HAS NOTHING TO DO WITH HOW
RICH OR POOR YOU ARE - THIS HAS NOTHING TO DO WITH MISINTERPRETATION
OR THE CORRECT INTERPRETATION OF THE DOCTRINE - THIS HAS TO DO WITH
WHO YOU ARE AND WHAT YOU WANT TO BE.

BLACKMAN - WHERE IS THE BLACKMAN.

WHERE IS THE BLACKMAN... THE REAL BLACKMAN...

I JUST HEARD... A FEW DAYS AGO... THE REAL BLACKMAN IS
TRYING TO GET HIMSELF TOGETHER... THEIR IS HOPE!

CASSANDRA

I AM THE QUEEN... CASSANDRA...
BESTOWED WITH THE GIFT OF PROPHECY
GOD HAS GIVEN THIS GIFT TO ME.
I REMAIN WITH PURITY...
THE QUEEN CASSANDRA...
THE ONE BESTOWED WITH THE GIFT OF PROPHECY
MY VISIONS SOME WERE UNTOLD, SOME REMAINED
AS IF UNTRUE
WHEN ALL OF IT CAME TO PASS THEY INDEED KNEW THAT I
AM CASSANDRA THE PROPHETIC QUEEN.
I WONDERED WHY MY MOTHER NAMED ME THIS, FOR NAMES
HAVE MEANING. THOUGH OFTEN SHE WOULD TELL ME
I HAD EYES IN THE BACK OF MY HEAD, THE THINGS I
WOULD MOSTLY SEE WOULD BE FROM THE EYES
IN THE FRONT OF ME.
WHEN I LEARNT OF WHAT MY MOTHER MET, THEN I
GREW TO UNDERSTAND THE SPIRITUAL GIFTS.
IT IS ONLY GOD THAT GIVES US THESE GIFTS.
AND IT IS LEFT UP TO US TO CHOOSE TO USE THEM
WISDOMLY.
FOR ONLY THROUGH OUR ACTIONS OF GOOD, WILL
GOD CONTINUE TO BLESS US AND KEEP US STRONG
THROUGH ALL THAT WE CAN NOT SEE.

DENNIS

As I sit here listening to George Fraser (author of success is in our race)
I hear some of your words!
I see some of you... a profile that spoke to success!
Indeed it was only a blessing that allowed me to partake
in the unfolding of who you were thought to be.
Your need to get involved in the community and effect change in
the lives of troubled adolescents. Was a need we both shared...
and it ignited our common belief. Your need to be independent and
a contributor to society in a positive manner... Was a need we both
shared and it ignited our common belief.
oh iWONDER what happened to you... to US.

Our journey began 1/1975...
Through the halls of Dekalb College, Saint Augustine's, Oglethorpe, Emory,
Clark, Atlanta University, Georgia State... oh iwonder what happened to US.

CONSTRUCTION...TRAINING...
Marta, The City of Atlanta, Dekalb County, Burger King, Fort McPherson, The State of Georgia...
Need I name more... A profile that spoke to success!
THOUGH THE DISSOLUTION BEGAN 11/1991...OUR HOME...A GOOD HOME!
THE THREE: Kassinda 3/80; Kameelah 2/85; Dennis 8/89; that came through US
DID... DO YOU REALLY CARE?
MAY THEY LEARN, SUCCEED, FLOURISH, FOR PLANTED WERE POSITIVE <u>SEEDS</u>.

%Arms outstretched involving and bringing some along. Helping those that are about to slip
through the net stay afloat.
Reach one teach one...% Oh how we used to sing.

I remember us exchanging those words...VOWS... IN 1976 and then again in 1977!

Gun Ho, energetic, ready to tackle every obstacle that came in a day. Nothing could divide US or stand in our
way... we are rough, we are tough, ain't going to take no stuff...

"DENNIS" ... DENNIS AND DENISE ...
oh I wonder what happened... to US. IT IS ONLY THE ALMIGHTY "I" CREATOR THE ALL-
IN-ALL THAT KNOWS THE TRUTH OF IT ALL.

The sacrifice...And how did we... maintaining a focus that we thought would never die!!
Understanding that the seeds sown would one day sprout...
and shortly blossom
What happened to you...to US...IT IS YOUR BELIEF IN YOUR ISLAMIC DUTY THAT HELPS TO
ANSWER THIS..
As I sat on that seat in 1994 I knew it was only LOVE that beckoned me to Let Go, and let you be who
you are to be.
I knew then that this division is dealt by GODS hand. AND therefore
I can accept divided we STAND.
I WISH YOU WELL AND MUCH SUCCESS -
THE MEMORIES WILL ALWAYS BE...WHETHER PAST OR PRESENT.
I WONDER what happened to you...!
THIS EXPERIENCE CREATES DISTANCE BETWEEN MANY LOVED ONES. I WONDER IS
IT WORTHY OF ACKNOWLEDGEMENT?
SOME CAN, SOME CAN'T, SOME WILL, SOME WON'T... DOES THIS STRENGTHEN FAMILIES?
THE EXPERIENCE SURFACED IN ME MY VIRTUOUS REALITY THEN
I REALIZED OUR PATHS WERE NOT TRUE DESTINY?

CROSSROADS

Life is full of crossroads...
decisions to be made...
decisions...
decisions...
decisions...
Each crossroad has two paths,
a good path,
a bad path,
Each of us must decide (decisions) which path to take (decide).
Each can take only one path... perhaps... at a time,
the good path,
the bad path.
Each have to decide, some in an attempt go from pillar to post, withering to and fro,
how indecisive sometimes trying to decide...the good path, the bad path.
Upon the good path more decisions belie (a waiting for each to decide).
Upon the bad path, how we are trapped, immersed in darkness, though
sometimes only to drift to and fro, instability and waywardness show...
decisions (only)... one each of us must choose to decide...
Hopefully the good path - HERE, each of us a go to the
EXTREME RIGHT >
EXTREME LEFT <
or middle course (path) - the balanced way –
each should decide.

Decisions...
Decisions...
Each must decide, for it is for each of us to travel the
decided path... only in hopes to work out our assigned (predestined/incarnated)
afflictions (trials, tribulations, karma... however you choose to define).

Each must CAREFULLY decide, why?
Because... until each work it (these) out each will return
again, again, and again, confronted with the same...afflictions...
only hopefully one day each decides to take the path... The eventual
return to the ULTIMATE ONE is ensured...
GOD - TRUTH - THE DIVINE ATONEMENT.
Which path shall you decide?
Decisions... Decisions... Decisions...
This time how shall you part, which affliction(s), trial(s) shall you have to confront, again,
again, again.

KING OF KINGS

YOU OH KING OF KINGS
GOD OF GODS (GOOD OF GOOD)
MESSENGER OF MESSENGERS
A TRUE EXAMPLE OF THE DARKER SKINNED MODELED MALE.
YOU REMAIN IN CONTROL, PURE, MEEKFULLY AND HUMBLY SO.
THE LIGHT FOREVER SHINETH FROM THY VESSEL AND FOREVER SHALL THE LIGHT
YOU BE.
IT IS FROM YOU THAT THE MISSION MUST CONTINUE. IT IS BECAUSE OF YOU THAT
THE MISSION IS.
YOU AN UPLIFTMENT TO THE MALES OF DARKER SKIN.. YOU GOING FORTH BEING
THE EXAMPLED MAN (MIND)
PORTRAYING THE ALL IN ALL (CREATOR) OF ALL THINGS WITHIN..
RELEASING THE SHACKLES AND CHAINS...ENSURING THAT THE DARKER SKIN MALE
RISES TO SUPREMANCY - THE REIGNING.
YOU CANNOT WAIVER, CANNOT BEND FOR YOU HAVE ALREADY GLIMPSED YOUR
DESTINY.
YOU ARE THE BRANCH, THE LIMBS AND THE VINES THERE UPON FOR IT IS YOU
THAT BEARS THE TRUTH.
DO NOT FORSAKE YOUR BROTHERS (MALE AND FEMALE) MY FRIEND. DO NOT
TRANSGRESS THE LAWS. THEY TOO ONE DAY WILL BE AS YOU FOR IT IS FOR ALL
TO ATONE.
THIS IS YOUR TIME AS IT IS MINE YOU ARE TO REMAIN TRUE AND THE
UNDERSTANDING IS OF YOU.
YOU ARE THE LIGHT OF LIGHTS AN IDEAL NOT YET TO BE REALIZED SO WISE,
YOUR STATURE WILL ALWAYS BE.
DISGRACE, DISHONOR, DISRESPECT ARE NOT OF YOU WHETHER YOU WALK IN THE
PRESCENCE OF THOSE OF MAN (MIND) OR THOSE OF UNSTABLE MATTER.
FOR IT IS ADAM (OSIRIS) AND EVE (ISIS) WHO LAID UPON US THESE IRRATIONAL
AND UNCONTROLLABLE BURDENSOME MOMENTS..
THE ALL-IN-ALL LAID UPON US NOT A BURDEN WE COULD BOT BEAR.
IT IS THE PRESENT DAY SAINTS AND SAINTESSES WHO DO NOT ALLOW
THEMSELVES TO BE CONQUERED OR CONTROLLED BY THE EVIL THAT LURKS
WITHIN...
BE NOT TAINTED, FOR THE TAMING (TEST) SOME WILL SUCCEED... SUCCEED SOME
WILL NOT, YOU CANNOT SUPPRESS YOUR INNER MOST FEELINGS, THE OUTER
SEEMINGS YOU CAN CONTROL.
THIS HOUSE (VESSEL, TEMPLE OF THE LIVING OMNIPRESENCE) SHALL SERVE THE
LORD, AND NOT CONNECT UNTIL IT IS WILLED BY THE CREATOR. FOR IT IS HE
THAT SAYS BE AND IT IS.
THOUGH SO CLOSE TO YOU A WEEVIL
YOU WITHSTAND AND SILENCE THE WICKED (WILD) HARLOT (MALE/FEMALE) OF
TODAY.
SUCCUMBING NOT, REMAINING PURE AND TRUE TO THE CAUSE.
YOUR SONS (MALE/FEMALE) WILL BE...FOR THEY CAN ONLY LIVE WHAT THEY LEARN.
STAY FORTH MY EXAMPLED MODELED DARKER SKIN MAN (MIND).
FOR IT IS YOU WHO ARE INDEED THE MESSENGER OF THE ALL-IN-ALL.
I AM THAT I AM

THE DISCERNMENT

LET ALL THAT HAVE EARS TO HEAR - HEAR
LET ALL THAT HAVE EYES TO SEE - SEE
HEAR WE MUST, SEE WE MUST, UNITED WE MUST BE.
IN THE LAST DAYS LIGHT WILL ATTRACT LIGHT AND BE... AS IT IS DISPOSED FOR
ALL OF GOD'S CHILDREN ARE COMING TOGETHER... IT SHALL BE.

GOD DISPOSES, THOSE OF CARNAL MIND PROPOSE.

DISPOSE - TO PUT IN CERTAIN ARRANGEMENT OR ORDER.
PROPOSE - TO OFFER

ANGELS DO NOT LIVE BY WHAT THOSE OF CARNAL MIND PROPOSE, ANGELS DO
NOT PROPOSE.
ANGELS LIVE ACCORDING TO WHAT GOD DISPOSES.

...ANGELS ARE INTUNE WITH GOD...

IT IS HE THAT SETS THINGS IN CERTAIN (PROPER) ORDER.

FOLLOW THE TRUE PATH (THE PATH OF THE FREE THINKERS, THE TRUTH
SEEKERS,
THE PATH OF THE GOD - THE DIVINE PATH)
FIND... ALL THINGS HAPPEN ACCORDING TO THE DIVINE PLAN AND WILL OF THE
TRUE AND LIVING GOD.

ANGELS OF GOD DO NOT PROPOSITION, ANGELS OF GOD ARE INTUNED WITH THE
GODLY REALM. UNDERSTAND AND KNOW, ANGELS OF GOD ACT ONLY
ACCORDING TO THE WILL OF GOD THE ALMIGHTY CREATOR OF ALL THINGS.

ANGELS OF GOD ARE WISDOM FILLED AND THEY ARE DIRECTED (GUIDED) BY THE
CREATING FORCE... THE ALL KNOWING.

YES! AMONGST YOU DWELL ANGELS... THE ULTIMATE REALITY IS A MYSTERY!

LET THERE BE LIGHT!
I AM THAT I AM!

IN SEARCH OF HIS BOYS

MY BOYS
  WHERE ARE YOU MY BOYS.
THE THREE OF YOU - WHERE ARE YOU.
MY HEART, MY SPIRIT IS WITH YOU - THIS WILL ALWAYS BE.
I MISS THE PHYSICAL TOUCH YOU SEE
I MISS THE THINGS WE USED TO DO... AND BE.
DADDY IS HERE FOR YOU...
WAITING ON THE PHONE TO RING, OR A PLEASANT VISIT FULL OF SURPRISE
   FROM MY THREE...
ARE YOUR NEEDS BEING MET, ARE THEY... IS THERE ANYTHING YOU DESIRE
   FROM ME.
I'M HERE WAITING YOU THREE WAITING FOR YOU AND ME
  TO BE... AGAIN FATHER & SONS.
ARE YOU BEING WELL CARED FOR, ARE YOUR NEEDS BEING MET - YOU
KNOW -
     LIKE DADDY DID THOSE THINGS.
HOW, IT WAS THEN... IS HOW I WANT IT TO BE.
   DADDY AND YOU THREE... THE LAUGHTER, THE CRIES
     THE BASKETBALL GAMES... THE WRESTLES AND TUSSELS DADDY
     MISSES YOU THREE.
RUN TO THE DOOR WHEN YOU HEAR ME, FROM WORK I COME HOME...
   UNLOCK THAT DOOR... LET ME GET TO MY BOYS - WHERE ARE YOU, YOU
     THREE...
OH! WHAT LOVE THERE IS... WAITING TO SHARE... WHAT DADDY HAS
BROUGHT FROM OUT THERE.
      MY BOYS... WHERE ARE YOU - YOU THREE.

LOVE AGAPE AND PHILEO

I FOUND LOVE BOTH AGAPE AND PHILEO...
      AT LAST...
I FOUND WHAT IS TRUE AND REAL.
THE COMPLIMENT THAT WE ALL ARE STRIVING FOR... SEARCHING...
      IF FOUND.
TO BE WHO WE ARE TO BE...
      THE ESSENCE OF BEING WITH AND STILL BEING WHO WE ARE -
          WHO WE STRIVE TO BE...
THE TRUTH... THE REAL...
BOTH AGAPE AND PHILEO.

LOVE, HONOR, HURT AND PAIN

THE ADAM SUFFERED, JESUS SUFFERED...
  MUSTAFA, BUDDHA, AND THE LIKE... ALL CAME TO SPREAD LIGHT...
     TO SPREAD LOVE... MUCH PAIN DID THEY BEAR,
         AGAPE... PHILEO...
THE LOVES THAT WE KNOW OF - FOR SOME HAVE EXPERIENCED ONE OR THE
OTHER... ONLY A FEW EXPERIENCE BOTH - THE ULTIMATE EXPERIENCE
AGAPE AND PHILEO - SYNERGIZED - TOGETHERNESS.
   THIS LIFE THE LIFE OF PAIN... OF SEARCHING...STRIVING...WANDERING...
     EXPERIENCE.

WITH OUR COMPLIMENT - WITH LIKE UNDERSTANDING, WITH THE LIGHT - LIKE -
     THAT ATTRACTS THE LIGHT -LIKE - (OUR COMPLIMENT) MAKES
     THE PAIN EASIER (SO MUCH) TO BEAR... NEEDLESS TO SAY MUCH
     MORE BEARABLE...

I FOUND, AT LAST, LOVE BOTH AGAPE AND PHILEO MY FRIEND.
YOU KNOW LIKE IT SHOULD BE.
    JUST BE - TO ME-
      WHAT'S TRUE AND REAL
       (AGAPE AND PHILEO)
        MY FRIEND.

PROFILE

A COMPLIMENT, COMPANION, A MATE
LETS AT <u>LEAST</u> HAVE A <u>FEW</u> THINGS IN COMMON
<u>*NOT MARRIED*</u> *IF HAS BEEN MARRIED HAS BEEN MARRIED ONLY ONCE, PLEASE*
NOT MORE THAN TWICE.
COMPASSIONATE
UNDERSTANDING
KNOWLEDGE BASE IN WORLD RENOWNED RELIGIONS
PHILOSOPHICAL YET SPIRITUAL
<u>*NOT OVERLY SEXED*</u>
<u>*KNOWS WHEN AND HOW TO BE ROMANTIC*</u>
MEDITATES
EDUCATED - AT LEAST A MASTERS DEGREE
<u>*CAN BE HUMBLE AND MEEK YET STRONG*</u>
LIKES: TRAVELING, TRAIL HIKING, BIKING, BOATING, FISHING, TENNIS,
CAMPING, HORSEBACK RIDING, THEATRE (PLAYS, OPERA), JAZZ, CLASSICAL
MUSIC, LIBRARY, CULINARY ARTS, ETHNIC ART, POETRY, READING, WRITING.
CAN PLAY A MUSICAL INSTRUMENT
CAN CARRY A TUNE
5'11 - 6'3 - 160-195LBS.
NO ROOMMATE
HAS HIS OWN PLACE (PREFERRABLY A HOUSE)
HAS STABLE JOB/LIKES TO WORK
WHITE COLLAR IS PREFERRED
DOES NOT MAKE LESS THAN $3,600.00/MONTHLY
FAMILY ORIENTED
LIKES CHILDREN
IF HE HAS CHILDREN, HE PROVIDES FOR HIS CHILDREN
SPENDS TIME WITH HIS CHILDREN
KNOWS HOW TO BE SOCIABLE
CAN COOK,
CAN CLEAN IF NEED ARISES
IS CLEAN
SECURE
SELF MOTIVATED
SELF SUFFICIENT
EFFICIENT/PROFICIENT
DOESN'T MIND HANDY WORK (PUTTING HANDS IN DIRT, PAINTING, CHANGING A
TIRE, ETC)
CAN DEAL WITH NOT BEING AROUND OR WITH SOMEONE ALL OF THE TIME
DOES NOT CARE FOR CLUBS OR DRINKING
DOES NOT DO DRUGS OR ALCOHOL
A LITTLE WINE IS TOLERABLE
CAN TALK INTELLIGENTLY AS WELL AS INTELLECTUALLY IF NEED ARISES
MAINTAINS PRINCIPLES BEFORE PERSONALITY
IS PRINCIPLED (MORALLY)
SELF WORTHY
A BUNCH OF ESTEEM
CAN DEAL WITH SPUR OF THE MOMENT CHANGES
A PARTNER IN EVERY SENSE OF THE WORD

JESUS THE MAN CALLED SAVIOUR

JESUS THE SAVIOUR THAT HIS NAME DOES MEAN
IN EVERY RELIGION HE DOES BE.
JESUS A JEW BORN IN BETHLEHEM OF JUDEA HIS MOTHER WAS A GIRL NAMED MARY.
JESUS THE CHRIST THE ANOINTED ONE OH HOW HIS MESSAGE MAKES US MERRY.

FOR EACH THAT CAME AFTER HIM HIS STORY WAS RETOLD

AND EVEN IN ISLAM THEY ACKNOWLEDGE HIM FOR IT IS JESUS ACCORDING TO HADITH A SECOND COMING HE WILL

JESUS KNEW THAT HE HIMSELF WAS NOT BUT A MAN FOR HE DID SAY MANY TIMES "THAT EVEN THAT THEY CALL ME CHRIST THIS BUT ONLY TELLS YOU THAT I AM UNIVERSAL LOVE".

FOR JESUS SO LOVED HIS CALLING, THAT HE DID SO WITHOUT CEASING.

MY INSPIRATION...

AS YOU THINK, YOU TRAVEL; AND AS YOU LOVE, YOU ATTRACT. YOU ARE TODAY WHERE YOUR THOUGHTS HAVE BROUGHT YOU; YOU WILL BE TOMORROW WHERE YOUR THOUGHTS TAKE YOU. YOU CANNOT ESCAPE THE RESULT OF YOUR THOUGHTS, BUT YOU CAN ENDURE AND LEARN, CAN ACCEPT AND BE GLAD.

YOU WILL REALIZE THE VISION (NOT THE IDLE WISH), OF YOUR HEART, BE IT BASE OR BEAUTIFUL, OR A MIXTURE OF BOTH, FOR YOU WILL ALWAYS GRAVITATE TOWARDS THAT WHICH YOU, SECRETLY, MOST LOVE. INTO YOUR HANDS WILL BE PLACED THE EXACT RESULTS OF YOUR THOUGHTS; YOU WILL RECEIVE THAT WHICH YOU EARN; NO MORE, NO LESS. WHATEVER YOUR PRESENT ENVIRONMENT MAY BE,

YOU WILL FALL, REMAIN OR RISE WITH YOUR THOUGHTS, YOUR VISION, YOUR IDEAL.

YOU WILL BECOME AS SMALL AS YOUR CONTROLLING DESIRE; AS GREAT AS YOUR DOMINANT ASPIRATION.

- JAMES ALLEN -

HONOR, GLORY AND PRAISE

TO THE ONE TRUE GOD, HONOR, GLORY, AND PRAISE.
THE CREATOR OF ALL THINGS AND OF ALL THE WORLDS
*IT IS ONLY **HE** THAT IS WORTHY OF PRAISE.*
IT IS HE THAT CALLED FORTH THE ANGELS,
AND UPON HIS PERMISSION IT IS HE THAT PERMITS US TO CALL ON THE
ANGELS
HE CREATED THE HEAVENS AND THE EARTH
HE PERMITS US TO CREATE
HE PROVIDES FOR US
HE CURES US
HE SUSTAINS US
HE GIVES US THE POWER TO CHOOSE
HE GIVES US THE POWER TO BE 'god' OVER OUR DOMAIN
THE ALL-IN-ALL

THE GREATEST GIFT

THE GREATEST GIFT YOU CAN GIVE MAN IS THE
GIFT OF DIRECTION.
THE ALMIGHTY CREATOR HAS GIVEN US A MAP TO BE USED FOR DIRECTION
AND GUIDANCE THIS MAP IS THE KEY TO HIS AND THROUGH HIS REALM.
WE ARE TO USE THIS MAP TO ASPIRE TO THE HIGHEST REALM, TO THAT
HIGHEST GLITTERING PEAK OF SUCCESS SPIRITUALLY, PHYSICALLY,
AND MATERIALLY
THE ABSOLUTE ALL HAS GIVEN YOU THE MAP TO THE KINGDOM
THE GREATEST GIFT.

Cassandra Huff

PERSEVERE

I SHALL PERSEVERE, MY FAITH,
HUMILITY,
RIGHTEOUSNESS
NEVER FAILS ME
I SHALL PERSEVERE ...!

THRIVING!

AS THE ROLLER COASTER COMES TO AN END, I STAND TALL AND
   SAY I AM THRIVING, I DON'T LOOK BEHIND, I ONLY LOOK
     AHEAD AND KNOW THAT THE TOTALS, MY FAVOR THEY ARE IN.
AS THE RESULTS OF THE TEST ARE COMPILED
AS THE FINAL TEST TELLS IT ALL
ONLY THE STRONG SURVIVE
ONLY THOSE THAT SURVIVE SHALL THRIVE.

Cassandra Huff

MY INSPIRATION...

LIKE UNTO A BEAUTIFUL WOMAN HIDDEN IN THE INTERIOR OF A PALACE WHO, WHEN HER FRIEND AND BELOVED PASSES BY, OPENS FOR A MOMENT A SECRET WINDOW, AND IS ONLY SEEN BY HIM; THEN AGAIN RETIRES AND DISAPPEARS FOR A LONG TIME; SO THE DOCTRINE SHOWS HERSELF ONLY TO THE ELECT, BUT ALSO NOT EVEN TO THESE ALWAYS IN THE SAME MANNER. IN THE BEGINNING, DEEPLY VEILED, SHE ONLY BECKONS TO THE ONE PASSING, WITH HER HAND; IT SIMPLY DEPENDS [ON HIMSELF] IF IN HIS UNDERSTANDING HE PERCEIVES THE GENTLE HINT. LATER SHE APPROACHES HIM SOMEWHAT NEARER, AND WHISPERS TO HIM A FEW WORDS, HER COUNTENANCE IS STILL HIDDEN IN THE THICK VEIL, WHICH HIS GLANCES CANNOT PENETRATE. STILL LATER SHE CONVERSES WITH HIM, HER COUNTENANCE COVERED WITH A THINNER VEIL. AFTER SHE HAS ACCUSTOMED HERSELF TO HIM FACE TO FACE, SHE ENTRUSTS HIM WITH THE INNERMOST SECRETS OF HER HEART.

VEILS (CURTAINS) ARE DIVISIONS BETWEEN THE SUPERCONSCIOUS THOUGHT OF GOD AND THE CONSCIOUS THOUGHT OF MAN.

THE WORDS OF SOD

UNEXPECTED CHANGES

THE CHANGES THAT COME THROUGH THE ACTIONS
OF OTHERS ARE OFTEN UNEXPECTED CHANGES
HOW SUDDEN, DIRECT, AND FORCEFUL ARE THESE
CHANGES AND HOW UNEXPECTEDLY PAINFUL TOO!,
HOW DARE YOU IN THE MIDDLE OF THIS ROAD DECIDE
TO MAKE AN UNEXPECTED CHANGE.
DON'T TURN ME OFF MY COURSE, YOU ARE GETTING READY
TO BIND ME AS WITH A CHAIN.
I'M NOT READY TO CHANGE MY COURSE OF LIFE,
AND FOR SOME REASON IT INCLUDES YOU.
WHAT HAPPENED TO ALL THE THINGS WE SHARED IN COMMON,
OR WERE THOSE JUST UNEXPECTED CHANGES THROWN IN
LIKE A MONKEYS WRENCH, EATEN UP WITH GULLIBILITY,
THAT COULD NOT BE SO FAR GREATER IS YOUR ABILITY.

I HAVE NOT FAILED TO LEARN ANY LESSON

MY FLOWER

AS PRETTY AS A FLOWER BLOSSOMING
AS PRETTY AS A FLOWER BLOSSOMING
AS PRETTY AS YOU CAN BE
BLOSSOMING
BLOSSOMING
BLOSSOMING
YOUR PETALS...
A SWEET PERFUME...
BLOSSOMING
BLOSSOMING
UNFOLD... TO WHO YOU ARE TO BE...
UNFOLDING
BLOSSOMING
MY FLOWER!

AS PRETTY AS YOU CAN BE...

FEELINGS

THESE FEELINGS TELL ME
WHAT ARE THEY
WHAT MAY THEY BE, FOR WHAT REASON ARE THEY TO BE.
TELL ME THESE FEELINGS WHAT ARE THEY...
THEY COME IN DIFFERENT SHADES, AND ACT IN DIFFERENT WAYS
(A SMILE, A LAUGHTER, A CHEER AND SOMETIMES A TEAR)
THESE FEELINGS WHAT ARE THEY
THEY GO AROUND, AROUND
UNDER, UNDER
DOWN, DOWN
UP, UP
SOMETIMES THEY COME AGAIN, AGAIN
AND IN DIFFERENT COLORS TOO
(ANGER, SADNESS, HATE, JOY, HOPE, PEACE, LOVE)
THESE FEELINGS TELL ME WHAT ARE THEY, ARE THEY
FEELINGS OR A PART OF MY PERSONALITY
FOR WHAT REASON HAVE THEY COME
TO VISIT ME THIS DAY.

WHEN THE SEASON IS RIGHT

Seasons... The joy of the seasons

the seasons as we know them are: WINTER, SPRING, SUMMER &FALL.

DURING EACH NATURE EVOKES AS WILLED...
  WHAT MANIFESTS IS THAT WHICH HAS EVOLVED
  FROM WHAT WAS EVOKED.
...OF WHATEVER IS...NATURE IS THE
CAUSE AND EFFECT OF ALL THAT EXISTS.
    NOTHING CAN TAKE ITS PLACE. WHEN THE SEASON IS RIGHT.
THE DESIRE TO BE DURING THE SEASONS RECEPTIVITIES...

THE CLOSER YOU ARE TO TRUTH, THE CLOSER YOU ARE TO HAPPINESS, THE CLOSER
YOU ARE... YOU ARE UNITED IN A PURE PREEMINENTLY GOOD PERFECTED STATE OF
MORALLY AND SPIRITUALLY SACRED PIOUS UNITY...
THIS QUEST IS NOT TOTALLLY IN VAIN...
FOR ONLY YOU KNOW FROM WHERE I AM COMING... AND WE DO NOT KNOW WHAT
  TOMORROW WILL BRING... LIFE... LASTING, INTERNALLY, FOREVER, ETERNALLY.

DO RE ME FA SOL LA TI

THE SEASONS ARE:

WINTER... THE COLD BREEZY DAYS... WANT TO SHARE THE GENTLE WARMTH OF
    SOMEONE WHO REALLY CARES.

SPRING... THE WARM BREEZES... WANT TO SHARE SOMEONE SO KIND AND CARING
    A HEART SO FULL OF TRUTH AND SUNSHINE... FROM THE SWING WE
    SHALL LAUGH AND SING "DO RE ME FA SOL LA TI" THE SEASON IS
    NOW... WINTER, SPRING, SUMMER, AND FALL...

WHEN THE SEASON IS RIGHT...

SUMMER... THE HOT BLAZING SUN... WANT TO SHARE A COOL, CHILLY LAUGHTER IN
    THE HOT SAND ON THE BEACH.

FALL... THE SCHEMEFUL COLORS FROM YOUR LAND TO MINE... WANT TO SHARE THE
    BLISSFUL COLORS OF THE RAINBOW (AURA) - RED, ORANGE, YELLOW, GREEN,
    BLUE, INDIGO, AND VIOLET - I'LL BE THERE FOR YOU AT THE BEGINNING AND
    END. WINTER, SPRING, SUMMER, FALL..

RIGHT IS SHARING, FOR THE SEASON IS RIGHT WINTER, SPRING, SUMMER, AND FALL,
  RIGHT IS SHARING FOR THE SEASON IS RIGHT DURING THEM ALL..

DO RE ME FA SO LA TI, THE TIME IS RIGHT, ALL SEASONS... WINTER, SPRING, SUMMER,
  AND FALL...

IN THE IMAGE OF GOD

IMAGE - WE ARE THE VIVID REPRESENTATION OF A WILL
OF A POWER, OF A DELIBERATE ACTION, OF A
COMMAND, OF AN ENERGY FORCE THAT HAS
CONTROL OVER ALL THINGS...
OF A FORCE THAT SAYS BE AND IT IS...
THAT FORCE WE KNOW AS
THE CREATOR OF ALL THINGS
THE ALL-IN-ALL

ALONE, LONELY

THERE IS A DIFFERENCE BETWEEN BEING ALONE AND BEING LONELY.
I DON'T MIND BEING ALONE I LIKE MY SPACE
    WHEN THE FEELINGS OF LONLINESS ARISE THEN I KNOW IT IS TIME
    FOR THE LONELY VOID TO BE FILLED.
    LONELINESS IS NOT FUN; IT BRINGS ABOUT FEELINGS OF PAIN...
    FEELINGS OF REJECTION...
ALONE I CAN BE... TO REMAIN LONELY
I DO NOT WANT FOREVER THIS WAY TO BE.

A MEETING

HE CALLED THIS MEETING, I WONDERED WHY
I WAS TRAVELING IN A HURRY ON THE FREEWAY TO GET
THERE ON TIME, WHY THIS MEETING I WONDERED WHY.

SO MANY DIFFERENT THOUGHTS RAN ACROSS MY MIND,
THIS MEETING I WONDER WHY.

WHEN I ARRIVED HE WAS STANDING ON THE BALCONY,
HE WANTED THIS MEETING, I STILL WONDER WHY.

Why

> *do I not bare the looks...*
> *do I not have enough ware...*

> *why.*

> *is it my attire or maybe the way my dark skin color appears*
> *am I a bit unpolished... or just a little bit to polished...*

> *why.*

do I not walk your talk... or just maybe I do not talk your walk

> *why.*

trying to figure it out

am I somebody in your eyes or am I nobody in your eyes...
how about only that, that helps you get by.

my self worth tells me to bid you bye, bye, not to hang around and
let my life pass me by.

DINNER FOR YOU

*MADE A NICE DINNER FOR YOU... THINKING YOU WERE ON
   YOUR WAY.
IT BOTHERS ME THAT YOU DON'T FOLLOW THROUGH WITH THE THINGS
   YOU SAY.*

*MADE A NICE DINNER FOR YOU...
   I HOPE TODAY YOU ARE HERE TO STAY.*

SUDDEN DISMAY

*as I sit waiting, wishing only at this time for a phone call... to let
me know that you are thinking of me... and soon will be on your way..*

got detained...

wanting so badly to be with you the initial vibrations I long to retain...

*wanting to share sometime with you, to cuddle, to caress, to hug, to
laugh, to smile, to chat*

and do all the things you would want us to...

*I look out the window what sudden dismay... the emptiness, the sadness,
the loneliness... how much longer before we connect,*

*wanting to share sometime with you, and do all the
things you would want us to.*

MISSING IN ACTION
(VIETNAM 1968-1970)

CSM WILLIAM H. HUFF IS HIS NAME,
AND MR. PRESIDENT HE IS MISSING IN ACTION.
WHERE IS MY DEDDY.
DON'T YOU REALIZE THAT HE HAS A WIFE WITH
8 CHILDREN AT HER BREAST, AND YOU SENT HIM OFF TO WAR.
THIS MISSING IN ACTION IS MAKING MY MAMA ILL
AND HARD TO REST.
FIND MY DEDDY HE'S OUT THERE IN THE COMBAT ZONES..
THE WEATHER IS DETERIORATING HIS BONES.
SEE MR. PRESIDENT HIS HELICOPTER WENT DOWN
TO THE GROUND, I'M TOLD.
I KNOW BY DAY AND BY NIGHT HE LIVES THE LORDS
PRAYER, THE LORD IS HIS SHEPPARD THIS I KNOW.
MR. PRESIDENT WHERE IS MY DEDDY DO YOU KNOW.
HE'S PROBABLY HAVING TO LIVE OFF OF THE
VEGETATION OF THE LAND. IS IT RAINING, SLEETING,
SNOWING. IS HE LYING ON THE WET GROUND,
TUCKED AWAY UP UNDER SOME BRUSH, OR IN
OPEN AMBUSH, ANSWER ME MR. PRESIDENT.
OVER 10,000'S OF MEN A CSM HE BECAME..
FIND MY DEDDY MR. PRESIDENT.
MR. PRESIDENT MY DEDDY'S MISSING IN ACTION.
HE'S #1, HE'S TOPS, HE'S A HERO. FOR THIS
COUNTRY HE IS RUNNING HIS BATTALION, AND
A GOOD JOB AT IT DOES HE.
NOW LET ME IMPART THIS BIT OF NEWS HERE.
I DON'T WANT NO TROUBLE OUT OF THE IRS OR
THE DEPARTMENT OF DEFENSE. MY DEDDY IS
SERVING HIS COUNTRY WELL FROM THE DAY THAT
MISSING IN ACTION...
HE IS FOUND EVERYTHING ON THIS EARTH SHOULD BE
FREE TO HIM.
HIS BODY WILL BE AILING AND DISABLING, SO DON'T
FORGET TO GIVE HIM HIS FULL SALARY AND 100%.
MY DEDDY, MR PRESIDENT, THAT'S WHO I'M
TALKING ABOUT, FIND HIM WON'T YOU PLEASE.

WE HAVE THE POWER

THE POWERS THAT BE...
I HAVE THE POWER...
YOU HAVE THE POWER...
WE HAVE (THE) POWER...
ENERGY - I, YOU, WE
VIGOR - FORCE -
STRENGTH –
ACTUALIZE...
THE POWERS THAT BE...
NINE...
ANGELS... OF ORDER... DIVINITY
THE POWER TO PRODUCE... PERFORM.
WE HAVE (THE) POWER
I, YOU, WE.

MY SPACE...version of

SPACE, SPACE, SPACE, SPACE, SPACE...
DISTANCE BETWEEN...
AAGH! I can breathe...
I can move freely...
I am continuously...
Space...
Boundless...
Space...
I'm within... I'm without...
SPACE - extending over and beyond... limitless...

My Space, My Space... Room to be me. AAGH!
I can breathe...

A (THE) MASON'S DAUGHTER

SHE IS A MASON'S DAUGHTER
  ALL THE KNOWLEDGE
SHE DID POSSESS WHILE SITTING
  UPON HIS KNEE.
HE WOULD READ AND STUDY THE SECRET ORDER
    A MASON IS HE
SHE IS A MASON'S DAUGHTER
    AND SUCH KNOWLEDGE SHE DOES POSSESS
IT IS THE SECRET ORDER THAT GAVE HER THE POWER.
THE POWER DOTH HER DIVINE PROTECTION BE.
SHE IS A MASON'S DAUGHTER, ORDAINED BY THE GOD.
BEAUTIFULLY SUBMERGED WITH THE DIVINE KNOWLEDGE.
THE KNOWLEDGE OF THE SECRET ORDER.
WHILE UPON HIS KNEE, HE STUDIED, IMPARTING
THIS KNOWLEDGE TO SHE.
HER GRACE, HER POISE, THE DIGNITY
REVEALED IS WHAT SHE POSSESSES
AS ORDAINED BY THE GOD...
SHE IS DIVINELY SO...
A MASON'S DAUGHTER...
THAT OF THE HIGHEST ORDAINED SECRET ORDER...

DOB...DOD
THE IN BETWEEN DASH

THE DATE OF YOUR ARRIVAL
MARKS THE DATE OF YOUR BIRTH...
SHOULD IT NOT BE THE DATE OF BEING.

THE DATE OF YOUR DEPARTURE
MARKS THE DATE OF YOUR DEATH...
SHOULD IT NOT BE THE DATE OF YOUR NEW DESTINY.

THE DASH IN BETWEEN...
THE IN BETWEEN DASH, FROM BIRTH... MILESTONES...
WE ENDURE...
JOYFUL, PAINFUL EXPERIENCES...
UNTIL THE DATE OUR NEW DESTINY ENDS... BEGINS ANOTHER
DASH - BETWEEN A NEW LIFE... A NEW DESTINY.
LIFE... INFINITELY... ETERNAL...
FROM THE DATE OF BIRTH... THE IN BETWEEN DASH
(EXPERIENCES)... TO THE DATE OF DEATH... OUR SOUL...
TRAVELS... ETERNALLY.

THE END OF THE RAINBOW

*THE END OF THE RAINBOW MARKS THE BEGINNING
OF ANOTHER BEGINNING.
THE RAINBOW IS ENDLESS, IT'S BOUNDARIES ...
LIMITLESS... INFINITELY...
HIDDEN ONLY BY THE SKIES BLUENESS...
THE ARC OF THE MOON... COLORFUL...
DURING THE QUIETNESS OF THE RAIN...
THE PEERING COLORS... ETERNAL
PEACE TO ATTAIN...*

*THE END OF THE RAINBOW,
ACHIEVED IS THE ATTAINMENT OF PEACE.*

HAVE YOU EVER THOUGHT

HOW IS THE CITY USING MY TAX DOLLARS
WELL...
DOWN AT THE CITY'S PERSONNEL DEPARTMENT [YOU KNOW
WHERE YOU PICK UP JOB APPLICATIONS].
THE CITY HAS...
A YELLOW APPLICATION.
IT HAS A PINK APPLICATION,
AND A GOLD APPLICATION,
HOW ABOUT A GREEN AND A BLUE ONE TOO!
LIKE SOMETHING YOU'D SEE AT A WEDDING OR A BABY SHOWER!!
THE JOB ANNOUNCEMENTS ARE COLORFUL TOO!

HAVE YOU EVER THOUGHT - WHY ALL THESE DIFFERENT COLORED
APPLICATIONS AND
JOB ANNOUNCEMENTS -
ARE THE TAXPAYERS TIRED OF WHITE AND BLACK.

COLORED COPIES THAT I KNOW OF COST 7.9 CENTS PER SHEET.
4.5 CENTS MORE THAN JUST A PLAIN WHITE AND BLACK COPY.
HAVE YOU EVER THOUGHT - WHY JUST PLAIN WHITE AND BLACK FOR
THE CITY WON'T DO.
WHY THE TAXPAYERS WANT OTHER THAN JUST PLAIN WHITE AND BLACK JOB
ANNOUNCEMENTS AND JOB APPLICATIONS. IS THE QUESTION NEEDING TO BE
ANSWERED.

I'M SO GLAD THAT I'M NOT A CITY TAX PAYING CITIZEN, CAUSE I'D
PROBABLY WANT THE 4.5 CENTS PER SHEET TO STAY IN MY POCKET -
AND DEFINITELY NOT END UP IN THE GARBAGE!

EVERY PENNY COUNTS!!

...THE CANDLE ONLY HE CAN LIGHT...

ON A LONELY HIGHWAY...
JUST THINKING HOW NICE IT WOULD BE FOR SOMEONE
SPECIAL TO ENTER MY LIFE AND LIGHT FOR ME A
CANDLE. WHILE ON THAT LONELY HIGHWAY MY
THOUGHT BECAME A REALITY... A CANDLE LIGHT WAS
LIT... BY THAT SPECIAL SOMEONE.
...THE CANDLE ONLY HE CAN LIGHT... IF FOR SOME
REASON THAT CANDLE LIGHT IS BLOWN OUT... I
WOULD QUESTION WHY. ONLY THIS SPECIAL SOMEONE
COULD RELIGHT THE CANDLE THAT HE LIT.
I WISH ONLY FOR THIS SPECIAL SOMEONE, AND HE
KNOWS WHO HE IS, TO LET THE CANDLE HE LIT IN 1995
REMAIN. IT IS NOW THAT THAT CANDLE LIGHT CAN
GIVE TO HIM A BETTER FLAME THAT WILL FOREVER
REMAIN THE SAME. THIS SURELY BRINGS LIGHT TO
MY LIFE.
IT IS MY DEEPEST WISH THAT HE CONTINUES TO
ALLOW THE FLAMING OF THE FLAMES THAT WE BOTH
KNOW EXIST. IT IS ONLY FOR HE THAT THIS CANDLE
WILL FLAME.
I'M WISHING UPON A STAR... ONLY FOR US TO BE...
THAT THE LIGHT OF THE CANDLE HE LIT IN 1995
CONTINUES TO FLAME. I'M WISHING UPON A STAR...
ONLY THAT THIS SPECIAL SOMEONE WILL LET THIS
CANDLE CLAIM FOR HE AND ME AN ETERNAL FLAME.
IT IS ONLY FOR HE THAT THIS CANDLE WILL FLAME.

"ALWAYS"
KID-O
CASSANDRA HUFF

I AM SHY... SO AM I

I AM SHY... SO AM I.

SITTING IN GREAT ADMIRANCE... LOOKING AT

EACHOTHER... OH WHAT PEACE...

NOT A QUESTION WHY.

I AM SHY... SO AM I.

MOMMY

*My mother is very nice. She has hair almost down to her
waist. She isn't as tall as Michael Jordan but she's kind of
tall. She hardly says profanity. She never screams when
she sees a spider or a snake all she does is kill it. She doesn't
buy me that many toys though.
But she is the best mother in the world.*

by Dennis Williams II

CHERYL WILLIAMS

TO KNOW HER IS TO DESCRIBE HER
SHE ENDURES MANY EXPERIENCES
TRIUMPHANT
SHE IS ONE OF STRENGTH
COURAGEOUS
SHE WEARS LIBERTY WITH VALOR
BOLD
SHE IS OF THE DARKER RACE
HERITAGE
SHE IS A NATURAL LEADER - WELL VERSED,
TALENTED, SKILLED.
WISE
HER COMMUNITY MEANS MUCH TO HER
CONFIDENCE
SHE TAKES THE YOUNG... AND PROVIDES AN
OPPORTUNITY... THAT THEY ONE DAY WILL UNFOLD
DEVELOPER
SHE IS ONE THAT CARES ABOUT ALL
GIVER
SHE IS A CARETAKE OF THE WOMB
MOTHER
POSITIVE INFLUENCE IS HER OUTER AND INNER
GARMENT
EFFECTUAL
SHE IS KEEN, SHE FEELS AND UNDERSTANDS WITH
DEEPEST SINCERITY AND EMPATHY.
SAGACIOUS
A DIVINE CREATION OF THE ALL-IN-ALL

We Thank You For Touching Our Lives

"Cassandra, Kassinda, Kameelah, & Dennis II"

Who Are You To Say It Matters

Who are you
What are you
Does it matter
What religion do you profess
Does it matter
I am a Creation of GOD
My relationship is with GOD
No man inspired religion can take GOD from me.
And this is what does matter.

When organized religion ceases to help the individual evolve into their true identity then it is time for the individual to move on.

All religions "ways of life" inspired from GOD, through man from GOD, serve a purpose.

Individual Evolution and an understanding of who we are, are to be, and who we have been... Once this is attained we can then begin to work out and grow through the errors that are presented in life without physical and mental struggle.

Throughout lifes journey this is GODS ultimate plan for each of us.

UNTITLED

"Women Recounting Experiences"

SHE AT 15 DID NOT KNOW AND WAS TAKEN ADVANTAGED OF. SHE RELIED UPON THE STRENGTH OF HER PARENTS TO ARRANGE IT ALL SO AT SUCH AN EARLY AGE SHE WOULD NOT BE BURDENED WITH A HUGE RESPONSIBILITY.

SHE AT 17 WAS VERY MUCH AWARE. BUT ONLY THOUGHT THAT HE WOULD HANDLE HER WITH UTMOST CARE.

SHE AT 19, HE WANTED HER... IT SEEMED SO PENETRABLY LIKE LOVE... IT WAS NOT SHE QUICKLY REALIZED.

SHE AT 21 COULD NOT BEAR THE THOUGHT OF NOT CONTINUING HER EDUCATION SO THERE WAS ONLY ONE THING SHE KNEW TO DO.

SHE AT 26 COULD NOT BEAR TO ACCEPT THE RESPONSIBILITY OF ANOTHER.

SHE HAS THREE... SHE LOVES THEM ALL SO DEARLY, HER EXPERIENCES ALLOW HER TO TEACH THEM ALL TO WELL.

IT TAKES TIME TO HEAL

HEALING IS A PROCESS
IT TAKES TIME TO HEAL
IT MAY TAKE TOMORROW,
OR THE NEXT DAY...
OR MAYBE A YEAR...
IT TAKES TIME TO HEAL.
LET ME HEAL TOTALLY...
SO I CAN BE WHO I AM TO BE
TO YOU AND ME.

IT TAKES TIME TO HEAL

HEALING IS A PROCESS
IT TAKES TIME TO HEAL
THE HEALING PROCESS CANNOT BE HURRIED
IT TAKES TIME TO HEAL
DON'T HURRY ME I WANT TO HEAL TOTALLY
I NEED TO EXAMINE WHAT HAS HAPPENED, I NEED
TO SEARCH FOR THE ANSWERS SO I WILL UNDERSTAND
DON'T HURRY ME
IT TAKES TIME TO HEAL
IT MAY TAKE TODAY, TOMORROW, OR YEARS TO COME.
THE PROCESS IS MINE. WHEN I HAVE HEALED I WILL
KNOW. DON'T TAKE THE PROCESS FROM ME LET ME
HEAL TOTALLY.
IT TAKES TIME TO HEAL.
HEALING IS A PROCESS... DON'T HURRY ME I WANT TO
HEAL TOTALLY, THEN I CAN BE WHO I AM TO BE.
I AM THAT I AM.

A DISTINGUISHED LOOK

HANDSOMELY GRAY HE IS. FROM HEAD TO TOE I
COULD THEN IMAGINE.
MASCULINED, GRACEFULLED, STATURED YOU COULD TELL.
SUCH A DISTINGUISHED LOOK. TO MYSELF I
THOUGHT...
I LOOKED... I LOOKED... AND I LOOKED... WHAT A VERY
UNUSUAL DISTINGUISHED LOOK. THE YOUTHFULNESS...
THE VIBRANCY... HANDSOMELY GRAY HE IS... AT SUCH
A YOUNG AGE... AND YES FROM HEAD TOE, I LEARNED.
HE'S BEEN GRAY SINCE A CHILD.
"I LIKE THE GRAY, IT'S YOU,
TO COLOR YOUR HAIR AND MUSTACHE TOO WOULD
TAKE AWAY FROM THE DISTINGUISHED, GRACEFULLED,
STATURED, MASCULINED MAN YOU ARE".
THE GRAY REPRESENTS WISDOM... IT IS SO NATURALLY
HIM, AND AN UNDERSTOOD BLESSING FROM GOD...
MY HANDSOMELY GRAY MAN HE IS... SECURELY
GROUNDED IN HIM.
SOMEONE TO SNUGGLE SECURELY WITH... SNUGGLE
SECURELY UNDER IF NEED BE TO DROWN MY SORROWS
IN... I KNEW THE MOMENT I MET HIM THAT HE IS THE
CHOSEN TO BE IN MY LIFE ETERNALLY.

An Everlasting Friend

He is Honest with me
This I appreciate
No promises does he make
"I'm not ready to make that commitment, you're moving to fast at the moment".
Words spoken with sincerity.
His matters, "I have things to resolve, if you can't wait I'll have to accept the fate.
He is an everlasting friend, honest about his matters.

In life you only have yourself to depend on, security you mustn't look for in anyone else. Always have the ability to take care of your responsibilities In his words it is revealed that he speaks from experience and wisdom.
An everlasting friend is what I consider him. The truth of the matter never let anyone down and never keeps anyone in bondage. The truth of the matter only sets you free.

He quickly learned of the elephants and mountains that I had to move, only one at a time could this be done. His words remain vividly in my mind and through the tribulations that apparently burdened me, I am strengthened to endure and persevere.

Don't depend on anyone else to give you what you need. Loud and clear is his message and for this I appreciate him as An Everlasting Friend.

Don't get caught up in another's emotions for surely your goals will get smothered - when emotions cease to allow who you are to flourish and evolve into your identity... you can't really define this as love.

Concentrate on getting your affairs in order, everything is in GODS hand... true love will be there for you, don't be sad because at this time there is no tangible action.
For in life there is but one guarantee... what is meant for you will be there awaiting at the end of the rainbow. Hold on to your vision for surely it is a reality. Loud and clear is his message and for this I appreciate him as An Everlasting Friend...

INTERVIEW ME FOR WHAT

OH! REALLY YOU WANT TO INTERVIEW ME.
INTERVIEW ME FOR WHAT.
COULDN'T YOU MAKE UP YOUR MIND BY READING MY RESUME AND RECOGNIZING WHO MY REFERENCES ARE.
OH! I'VE ALSO INCLUDED A BIOGRAPHICAL SKETCH - HOW PERSONAL CAN I GET.
CAN'T YOU READ AND TELL WHO I AM. WHAT I CAN DO, AND WHO I CAN BE.

TRYING TO LOCATE A JOB IS A JOB IN ITSELF. SHOULDN'T MY QUALIFICATIONS SPEAK FOR THEMSELF. INTERVIEW ME FOR WHAT.

DOES MY PROFILE FIT IN YOU COMPANY'S... LOOK MADAME OR SIR, ARE YOU LOOKING TO HIRE SOMEONE WITH SHORT HAIR OR LONG, OBESE OR UNDERWEIGHT, GOOD LOOKING OR NOT, MY QUALIFICATIONS ARE WHAT WILL BRING PROFITS TO YOUR ORGANIZATION.

CAN'T JUST BE PRETTY, JUST BE QUIET, SIT AND PRETEND - A LONG WITH THOSE LOOKS AREN'T YOU LOOKING FOR SUBSTANCE. LOOK JUST PITCH ME UP AN OFFICE OVER THERE TO THE SIDE. LET ME START WORKING YA' HEAR, I'M A VALUABLE ASSET.

THE HANDSHAKE - UP ONCE, DOWN ONCE - MY RIGHT HAND I EXTEND TO YOUR RIGHT. A FIRM GRIP TELLS A LITTLE SOMETHING, BUT MY QUALIFICATIONS TELL IT ALL.

MY SKILLS ARE TRANSFERRABLE. KNOWLEDGE, SKILLS, EXPERIENCE, I'M NOT LACKING EITHER OF THESE BASED ON MY QUALIFICATIONS APPOINT ME A JOB PLEASE.

ALL THESE IDIOSYNCRACIES - LIKES AND DISLIKES. LET'S JUST DEAL WITH WHAT WE ARE HERE FOR. ONE GOAL TO PRODUCE OUTCOMES AND RESULTS. SERVICE PLEASE, THAT IS THE KEY.

BE HUMANE, I NEED A JOB. BEING DIVORCED WITH 3 MOUTHS TO FEED SURELY TELLS YOU I HAVE ONE FOCUS IN MIND. THIS REASON AMONGST OTHERS MAKES ME RELIABLE, FLEXIBLE, DEPENDABLE, AND A TEAM MEMBER (PLAYER)... WELL MY QUALIFICATIONS TELL YOU I'M WILLING, ABLE, READY AND AVAILABLE.

I REMAIN HUMOROUS THROUGH IT ALL, BUT BELIEVE YOU ME ALL THESE INTERVIEWS, APPLICATIONS AND RESUMES... THE EXPENSE INCURRED... PLEASE BASED ON MY QUALIFICATIONS AND REFERENCES, JUST APPOINT ME A JOB... JUST MATCH ME UP DON'T TRY TO FIT ME IN... YOU WON'T REGRET IT IN THE END. I'M A VALUABLE ASSSET. OUTCOME AND RESULTS. I'M IN.

...THE INTERVIEW...

THE FIRST INTERVIEW IS THE LASTING IMPRESSION.
ISN'T THAT WHAT WE HAVE ALWAYS BEEN TOLD.
OH! REALLY THEN WHY THE SECOND, THIRD, FOURTH, FIFTH, AND SOMETIMES SIXTH INTERVIEW.
COULDN'T YOU MAKE UP YOUR MIND AFTER THE FIRST...LASTING IMPRESSION... INTERVIEW.

THE APPLICATION/RESUME' IS FOR YOUR USE, SHOULD YOU WANT TO VERIFY THE TRUTH.
LOOK! HONESTLY, WHEN DO I HAVE TIME TO FIND OUT ALL SORTS OF THINGS ABOUT YOUR COMPANY. I'M APPLYING FOR A POSITION BASED ON A JOB POSTING.

SHOULDN'T MY QUALIFICATIONS SPEAK FOR THEMSELF.

THAT FIRST...LASTING IMPRESSION...INTERVIEW SHOULD HAVE TOLD IT ALL. FOR WHAT REASON DID I NOT QUALIFY FOR THIS JOB. ANSWER ME PLEASE WITH A CALL. TRYING TO LOCATE A JOB IS A JOB IN ITSELF. IN THIS JOB YOU DON'T GET PAID AT ALL.

DOES MY PROFILE FIT IN YOUR COMPANY'S... LOOK MADAME OR SIR, ARE YOU LOOKING TO HIRE SOMEONE WITH SHORT HAIR OR LONG, OBESE OR UNDERWEIGHT, GOOD LOOKING OR NOT. MY QUALIFICATIONS ARE WHAT WILL BRING PROFITS TO YOUR COMPANY...
OR IS THIS JUST A MYTH... FROM ONE AGENCY TO ANOTHER AGENCY.

I KNOW ABOUT THE AGENTS THAT SIT IN AND TRY TO PREVENT SOMEONE FROM BEING HIRED. ALL IN AN EFFORT TO KEEP EVERYTHING WITHIN. THERE IS ALWAYS ROOM FOR NEW BLOOD, ESPECIALLY AN ASSSET THAT'S INVALUABLE.

CAN'T JUST BE PRETTY, JUST BE QUIET, SIT AND PRETEND.. ALONG WITH THOSE LOOKS AREN'T YOU LOOKING FOR SUBSTANCE.
THE HANDSHAKE - UP ONCE, DOWN ONCE - MY RIGHT HAND I EXTEND TO YOUR RIGHT. A FIRM GRIP TELLS A LITTLE SOMETHING, BUT MY QUALIFICATIONS TELL IT ALL.

MY SKILLS ARE TRANSFERRABLE. KNOWLEDGE, SKILLS, EXPERIENCE, I'M NOT LACKING EITHER OF THESE. BASED ON MY QUALIFICATIONS APPOINT ME A JOB PLEASE.

BE HUMANE, I NEED A JOB. BEING DIVORCED WITH 3 MOUTHS TO FEED SURELY TELLS YOU I HAVE ONE FOCUS IN MIND. FOR THIS REASON, AMONGST OTHERS RELIABLE, FLEXIBLE, DEPENDABLE, AND A TEAM MEMBER (PLAYER) I AM... WELL MY QUALIFICATIONS TELL YOU I'M WILLING, ABLE, READY AND AVAILABLE. I REMAIN HUMOROUS THROUGH IT ALL, BUT BELIEVE YOU ME ALL THESE INTERVIEWS, APPLICATIONS, RESUMES... THE EXPENSE INCURRED... PLEASE BASED ON MY QUALIFICATIONS AND REFERENCES JUST APPOINT ME A JOB...

JUST MATCH ME UP DON'T TRY TO FIT ME IN... YOU WON'T REGRET IT IN THE END.

THE TRUTH OF THE MATTER

AT 10, A CHILD OF EIGHT, HER MOTHER BEGAN WITH AN ILLNESS. MANY DAYS WHILE ALL THE OTHER 10 YEAR OLDS WERE PLAYING, HER ONE YEAR OLD SISTER SHE WAS STROLLING AND TAKING CARE OF.

FROM AGE 10 TO JUST A FEW MONTHS AGO...THOUGH HIGHLY INTELLIGENT SHE IS...
SHE WORKED MANY HOURS CHARITABLY AND MANY MORE HOURS FOR A VERY LOW PAY. SHE WEARS THE VIRTUE CHARITY PROUDLY...NOT PUFFED UP...THE GREATEST GIFT OF ALL.

EVERYTHING SHE HAS ACQUIRED... TOOK PERSEVERANCE AND HARD WORK.

SHE IS WITH THE UNDERSTANDING THAT HER DUES HAVE BEEN PAID. UNQUESTIONINGLY... SHE UNDERSTANDS WHAT HER PURPOSES HAVE BEEN... SHE HAS EVOLVED TO UNDERSTAND WHAT HER PURPOSE NOW IS..

IT WOULD BE UNFAIR TO HER AND A WASTE OF TIME "YOURS AND MINE" TO REPEAT WHAT SHE HAS EVOLVED THROUGH.

SHE MUST BE WISE IN HER CHOICES.

AS SHE REMAINS IN TACT TRUE TO HER GODSELF,
SHE IS COMFORTABLE IN KNOWING THAT WHEN ONE DOOR IS CLOSED ANOTHER IS OPENED... SOON WHAT SHE DESIRES WILL BE.

SOLDIER BORN

BE STRONG - ALL OF US ARE SOLDIER BORN.

WE CAN ROLL WITH THE PUNCHES, AND GLIDE THROUGH THE CHANGES HOLD BACK THE TEARS, DON'T YOU CRY, WE HAVE GOT TO PACK OUR BAGS A NEW STATION IS WAITING FOR US TO ARRIVE.

BUT! DEDDY I'M TIRED, WE'RE TIRED, WE DON'T WANT TO TRAVEL NO MORE, CAN'T WE FIND A PLACE TO CALL OUR HOME.

MOMMY, "I JUST MET KATHY AND MARY TOO", IF WE LEAVE I'LL NEVER SEE OR HEAR FROM THEM AGAIN.

"I KNOW DEAR. I KNOW SWEATIE, BUT THIS IS DEDDY'S CAREER. WHEN UNCLE SAM COMES A CALLING WE HAVE TO PACK OUR BAGS AND START A SAILING.

BUT DEDDY, MOMMY IS ILL - UP TO TRAVELING SHE IS NOT... HONEY! MY FAMILY I HAVE TO KEEP TOGETHER.

TO KEEP TOGETHER, CAN'T LEAVE YOU ALL BEHIND. WITH ME YOU MUST BE. BE STRONG NOW ALL OF YOU ARE SOLDIER BORN. WHEN UNCLE SAM COMES A CALLING, PACK OUR BAGS WE MUST, A SAILING WE GO FOR A NEW STATION IS WAITING FOR US TO COME.

MOMMY WILL BE FINE, I WILL GET THE BEST OF CARE FOR HER, MY SOLDIER BORN TROOP WILL NOT GO FOR NEEDING A THING, WITH DEDDY YOU ALL WILL BE,

HOLD BACK THE TEARS DON'T YOU CRY. OFF TO TRAVELING THE WORLD WE WILL SEE.

OKAY, DEDDY. A SHIP, A PLANE, A TRAIN - THE QUEASY STOMACHS, THOSE LONG CAR RIDES. MOMMY, DEDDY WHEN WILL IT END, IS THIS THE WAY MY LIFE HAS GOT TO BE EVERY 2-3 YEARS ANOTHER STATION.

THE NEW FACES, THE NEW PLACES, AND YOU SAY SECURITY, STABILITY, STRENGTH ARE BEING CREATED IN ALL OF US. I'VE BEEN SHIFTED HERE AND THERE EVERY 2, 2 1/2, 3 YEARS PRACTICALLY. ONE THING I HAVE LEARNED FOR SURE I CANNOT ACCEPT ANYTHING.

A SOLDIER YOU ARE - AND SOLDIER BORN WE ARE - WITH ONE FOCUS, AND THAT IS TO SERVE OUR COUNTRY.

THE MANY RELIGIONS... HOW DIFFERENT... SOME SIMILAR THOUGH... WHAT RELIGION WILL THIS CHAPLAIN HERE PROFESS. MY DOG TAGS READ PROTESTANT, BAPTIST, METHODIST... WHICH ONE AM I REALLY, TELL ME DEDDY SO I'LL KNOW SHALL I COURTESY, BE SPRINKLED, OR EMERGED IN A POOL, WHAT KIND OF BAPTISM WILL IT BE THIS TIME. DO YOU KNOW. SHALL I EAT THIS BREAD OR DRINK THIS AS A SYMBOL OF HIS BLOOD, IT SEEMS AS IF THEY ALL TEACH OF JESUS...

WAS JESUS A PROTESTANT, BAPTIST, OR METHODIST. COME ON DEDDY HELP ME TO DECIDE, I'M TIRED OF THESE CRACKERS AND GRAPE JUICE, A SYMBOL... WHAT DO THESE REPRESENT.

SOLDIER BORN

THE NEW FACES, NEW CULTURES, IT'S NICE TO BE ABLE TO HAVE A WORLD VIEW ALL THESE DIFFERENT ETHNICITIES. MY MOTHER IS GERMAN, JAPANESE, KOREAN. MY FATHER IS BLACK, WHITE... OKAY. THIS IS A MELTING POT... I LEARNED THAT IN WORLD HISTORY... BUT LET US NOT FORGET THE MAIN REASON WE ARE HERE.

WE ARE REPRESENTING OUR COUNTRY. SOLDIER BORN WE ARE. HEY MY DEDDY IS A BLACK SOLDIER SERVING HIS COUNTRY, AND WHENEVER UNCLE SAM COMES A CALLING, WE PACK OUR BAGS, AND A NEW STATION WE GO TO A SAILING. BY PLANE. TRAIN, SHIP, OR CAR.

THE BEST OF EVERYTHING IS WHAT I'M ACCUSTOMED TO SO I JUST CAN'T ACCEPT JUST ANYTHING.

I MAY NOT REMEMBER THE GERMAN LANGUAGE I LEARNED JUST A FEW YEARS AGO BUT I WILL ALWAYS REMEMBER BEING THE ONLY "ONE" IN SOME OF MY CLASSES.

TO KEEP US ABREAST OF OUR HISTORY YOU PROVIDED US WITH LITERATURE ON BLACK HISTORY AND CURRENT EVENTS.

IF YOU COULD YOU MADE IT POSSIBLE FOR US TO STAY A NIGHT OR TWO WHERE YOU AND MOMMY WERE BORN AND RAISED, ALL IN AN EFFORT TO KNOW THE RELATIVES THAT I WILL PROBABLY NOT EVER BOND WITH.

THEY TELL ME DIVERSITY IS THE KEY. ALL THIS DIVERNESS. ALL THIS EDUCATION ALL THIS KNOWLEDGE AND TRANSFERRABLE SKILLS, AND FLEXIBILITY. WHO WILL I BECOME.

SOME HAVE CALLED ME SNOWFLAKE, OREO, BLACK/WHITE GIRL. HEY FARAH FAWCETT IS THAT REALLY YOUR HAIR.

HOW IGNORANT SOME OF US REMAIN.

OH THE SCARS THAT I MUST WEAR. I WONDER WHY.
UNCLE SAM DOES NOT MAKE IT EASY FOR THOSE WHO ARE SOLDIER BORN THE DIFFICULTY WE SOMETIMES MEET TO SECURE AN EDUCATION AND EMPLOYMENT SO THAT A DECENT LIFE WE CAN PROVIDE.

OH THE SCARS THAT I MUST WEAR.
I'M A MILITARY VETERAN DEPENDENT. CAN I HAVE SOME POINTS FOR THIS ON MY JOB APPLICATION AND JOB TESTING. GIVE ME SOME VETERANS PREFERENCE PLEASE. APPOINT ME A JOB. JUST MATCH ME UP. DON'T TRY TO FIT ME IN.
YOU WON'T REGRET IT IN THE END.

SOLDIER BORN

I AM SOLDIER BORN, DON'T I CRY.
WHEN UNCLE SAM CAME A CALLING WE PACKED OUR BAGS,
IT WAS TIME TO GO A SAILING, BY A PLANE, A TRAIN, A SHIP,
A CAR WHERE ARE MY POINTS. COUNT ME IN PLEASE.

OH THE SCARS THAT I MUST WEAR.
BE STRONG YOU ARE SOLDIER BORN
1951 - CHARLES GARRETT
1953 - WILLIAM EUGENE HUFF
1955 - WILLIAM HOWARD HUFF, JR.
1956 - CASSANDRA DENISE HUFF
1958 - DAPHNE ALINE HUFF
1960 - LUVENIA WILLENE HUFF
1961 - REGINA LOUISE HUFF
1962 1963 - ANITA CYNTHIA HUFF
1963 1965 - ARLENE LESLIE HUFF

I Wrote a poem today, especially for you...

Blue Jay...
you just keep flying in my yard, and you sit there perched...
(as if inspecting)... ...guarding me.
I know who sent you. It was Red Bird. Sometimes ago, I told
Red Bird to bring you to me... You were sent right this way.
                    Blue Jay -

          Blue Jay -
          A road runner are you.
Time to slow down. Time to stop running up and down those roads...
Blue Jay... Blue Jay... My wish has come true.
          I know you are here today to stay...
... Concrete Substance.

          "Kid-o"

"Blue - represents the highest ideals of truth (true blue), loyalty, trust and devotion. Blue conveys wisdom, serenity, peace, patience, gentleness, honesty, sincerity, reliability, creative self-expression and communication, coolness and calmness, soothing to the mind and emotions, excellent in times of stress, anxiety, fear and panic, poise, inner power, contemplation, meditation, attunement with spirit, vitality, growth.

"Red - strength, confidence, courage, will power, determination, motivation, honor, integrity, independence, optimism, hope cheerfulness, cope with life, meet challenges, alertness, initiative, leadership, authority.

The Legion of Light The Benefits and Psychology of Colors

PARENTS, TEACHERS ARE PARENTS TOO!

Parents and teachers have such a huge responsibility. Both are the tree(s), and the children are the fruit. Some teachers eat while they work, some I'm sure fast, eating crackers and drinking water through the day being fair to all whether red, yellow, black or white — handling the day sometimes under much distress, at times eustress. Some parents, teach (reinforce), fast and pray hoping that their children achieve academically, morally, and principally. In observation, some teachers try to teach; baby sit; and remold. Wow! teachers are you paid enough for this huge responsibility — of a burden.

A parent, teacher, social worker, psychologist, counselor, administrator too! All of them You Are. Parents/Teachers plant more than one good seed so more than evil they (our children) will be. Remember Henry Van Dyke's words: "The best rose bush, after all, is not that which has the fewest thorns but that which bears the finest roses."

His words are saying it's not the number of mistakes one makes but the end result of the final transformation. Let us be good role models, continually sowing good parental and educational seeds. Ensuring as our children endure these units of education and family, that the chances of them becoming more good than not are greater while they evolve into their knowingness.

Sometimes off the path we all may wander, however holding on to the good seeds that are sown we by faith continue to believe that the fruit will not fall to far from the tree. The fruit (our children) will not wander to far from their role models, hopefully. The foundation once laid and engraved cannot be taken from them. The bad, naughty, naughty not on today, can evolve into being good almost every day. The good let us all help keep them this way.

With good all things (good) are possible. Know that during all the trials and tribulations that they might be presented with, we can help them endure by being uplifting, inspirational, positive, constructive, enriching role models. Teaching them along the way to hold on to The Good That is Within. We are not to steal their creativity, dignity, or their souls, we are only to enhance and enrich them academically, morally, principally preparing them for the tomorrows that will come.

Help Them Be What They Are To Be In Good Godly Form.

Love to All Humankind.

Written by Author Cassandra Huff of Decatur, DeKalb Georgia while volunteering at Avondale Elementary School in the spring of 1999.

Heritage...

I am embraced... I am encouraged... I am hopeful...
I am esteemed... I am Me... My Heritage...
My forefathers... Foremothers... our Heritage...
I am embraced... I am encouraged... I am hopeful...
the dignity the pride...
... the womb... of civilization... of the
beginning... Heritage... cultures... traditions...
ancestors...
In me... secretly... evasively... they hide...
From where Have I come... Who are these (they) that lie within Me.
One at a time do we learn of each... In you (me) ... they hide...
Heritage... Dignified... Proud... Uplifting... Motivating...
My Heritage... as defined...
we all wear... masked... revealed...
revealed... Characteristics... Personalities...
engrained...
I am Me... My Heritage... I wear it Proudly...

-CEDAR GROVE ELEMENTARY K5 AWARDS PROGRAM-

"CEDAR GROVE ELEMENTARY A PLACE WHERE HOPE BEGINS AND DREAMS COME TRUE"

WAGNER BERNARD HUFF

AUNTEE WONDERED IS MY LIL! NEPHEW GOING TO MAKE IT TO THE PLACE WHERE HOPE BEGINS AND DREAMS COME TRUE ON THIS 5TH DAY OF JUNE 1998.
WITH WORRIES OF ME AND IF I WAS GOING TO BE ALIVE FOR THIS DAY. YOU LIKE ALL THE OTHER STUDENTS MADE IT HERE TODAY. I AM GRATEFUL. I AM THANKFUL. AS I SIT AND WATCH THE ALMOST 160 STUDENTS - OUR FUTURE. THESE ARE THE WORDS THAT COME TO MIND.
    ALL THESE BRIGHT AND FASCINATING CHILDREN. COUNT THEM
    1 - ALMOST 160. JUST SIX CLASSES. MY A TEACHERS JOB... PARENTS,
    COUNSELORS, ADMINISTRATORS, SOCIAL WORKERS, PSYCHOLOGISTS...
    A FRIEND. TEACHERS ARE ALL OF THEM. A COMMUNITY FOR ONE FOR
    ALL WAGNER AUNTEE IS PROUD OF ALL OF THE STUDENTS.
    THE COLORS THEY ARE DRESSED IN: RED, WHITE, GOLD, PINK, BEIGE,
    BLACK, BROWN, YELLOW.
    GOSH! ALL THESE FASCINATING AND BRIGHT CHILDREN. MY THE TASK EVEN
    PARENTS HAVE TRYING TO KEEP THEIR OWN CHILDREN ON TRACK. THE RIGHT
    PATH WE MUST TEACH THEM TO TROD.

DID EACH STUDENT GET ACQUAINTED WITH ONE ANOTHER. DID YOU GET ACQUAINTED WITH ALL OF THEM. WONDER WHAT THEY WANT TO BE WHEN EACH OF THEM GROW UP!

THE PLEDGE OF ALLEGIANCE... GOD BLESS AMERICA CONTINUALLY... A FEW 15 MINUTES LATE THE PROGRAM DID START. WHO CARES. IT WAS ON TIME TO ME. MAYBE THEY SHOULD ESTABLISH A SCHOOL PER WAY OF LIFE. AND LET CEDAR GROVE ELEMENTARY AND CEDAR GROVE HIGH SCHOOL BE THE PILOT PROJECTS. UTILIZING STUDENT TEACHERS. CUT OUT SOME OF THIS MISERY.

IT'S THE OUTCOME OF THE EFFORTS. TEACH THE STUDENTS TO APPLY THEMSELVES AND TO DREAM EFFECTIVELY. EACH OF YOU - CLASS OF 2010. YOU ARE YOU, AND YOU ARE YOU... JUST BE WHAT YOU WANT TO BE POSITIVELY! WAGNER YOU MADE IT HERE TODAY, FOR YOU K-5 AWARDS PROGRAM. THOSE LONG NIGHTS AND SLEEPY A.M.'S WHY DON'T THEY HAVE SCHOOL. DAY AND NIGHT TO FIT EVERYONES SCHEDULE. HA! HA!

MS. SANDERS ANDMS. GURLEY MY HAT IS OFF TO BOTH OF YOU. YOU BOTH ARE TO BE COMMENDED FOR A JOB WELL DONE. AS ALL TEACHERS, MORE THAN TEACH THEY HAVE TO. ALL OF YOU ARE SPECIAL!!

JAMES AKINS	*KAMESIA BURNEY*	*JUELISA FLAGG*	*WAGNER HUFF*
VANN BURNETT, JR.	*VEONDUS DENNIS*	*JOHN GOODSON*	*DERRICA JACKSON*
RYAN EUBANKS	*RASHANNA DINGLE*	*DWAN HENRY*	*DIAMOND JAMES*
BRANDON GLEATON	*JAMEL DOBBS*	*BENNY HOOD*	

PERSTEPHANIE MANNING

NAEEM PATTERSON   *QUANIQUA EPPS*   *BRANDON HOWARD*

RABIYA MINOR

CHELSEA MOORE   *KOURTNEE MORRIS*   *ALEXANDDRIA PRITCHETT*
REBEKAH RACHELS   *PORSCHE REED*   *ACCIRE ROBINSON*   *SHAKEIRA WEAVER*
JALEEL WOODS... CONGRATULATIONS! TO ALL OF THE CLASSES OF 2010 CEDAR GROVE ELEMENTARY...!!!!!!!!!!

"The Mind"

Dedicated to the One and Only

And I caught...
me a boldacious (courageous) Black & Gold
Butterfly. He flew right into my yard...
He is here to stay...
Come here to me you Butterfly ...
A change is surely a coming... to stay.
You handsome Black & Gold Butterfly...
Be Ye' Transformed...
The Renewed You [ ]
"The Mind."

**** *emerged in a butterfly* ****

THE GEM

THE GEM THAT I KNOW REPRESENTS
    TRUTH AND FRIENDSHIP
      IN ALIGNMENT IT MUST BE. WHATEVER IT MEANS
TO YOU DOES NOT MATTER, FOR I KNOW WHAT
        IT MEANS TO ME.
I KNOW IT IS AN ORIGINALITY,
      THIS IS A REALITY THAT WILL ALWAYS
        BE A PART OF ME.
THOUGH TO ME THIS GEM'S TRUTH AND MEANING IS
    SHEER ITS INNER DIMENSION IS HARD TO PEER, FOR
    IT RISES TO HEIGHTS UNKNOWN AS SCRIPTURED
THAT ALL OF US CAN. THERE IS NO MATCH OR EQUAL, FAR OR NEAR. YOU MAY NOT FIND A GEM LIKE THIS EVER AGAIN, AS ITS GOODNESS IS FROM GOD. WHAT IT APPEARS TO BE DOES NOT MATTER BECAUSE I KNOW THIS GEM IS A GEM. WE ARE TOLD BE ALL AND WHAT WE WANT TO BE, AND THIS IS ONE GEM THAT WILL TAKE YOU TO THAT HEIGHT. I'VE ATTACHED TO THIS GEM AND I CAN'T LET GO. GARNET IS A GEM, I RECOGNIZED THE DEPTH OF THIS GEM WHEN I FOUND IT BURIED DEEPLY IN THE SAND. THE MOMENT I SAW IT IN ITS GLEAM AND BRIGHTNESS CAUSED ME TO GLOW AND KEPT ME GLOWING ETERNALLY. THIS GEM BRINGS LOVE AND COMPASSION AND ITS STRENGTH IS TO PURIFY, AND THAT SPECIAL TOUCH, I DON'T MIND TELLING ANYONE THIS GEM KNOWS HOW TO BRING HARMONY. THE TRUTH AND FRIENDSHIP IT REPRESENTS IS OFTEN UNEASILY FOUND. YOU MAY NOT KNOW ITS EVERY MOVE BUT BELIEVE ME NO DECEIT IS INVOLVED. THIS IS ONE GEM I ALWAYS WANT AROUND. WHETHER SPIRITUALLY, ETHERICALLY, OR PHYSICALLY IT NEVER DEPARTS FROM ME.

    IT IS A GUIDING LIGHT THAT I WILL ALWAYS WELCOME. ITS COLOR TO ME IS A DEEP TRANSPARENT RED, A COURAGEOUS BEING THAT IS HARD TO SEE THROUGH. THIS GEM HELPS TO KEEP YOU HONEST AS A MATTER OF FACT. BUT YET SINCERELY CONCERNED, AND CARING WITH A SMOOTHINESS ABOUT ITSELF, ALTHOUGH AROUND THE EDGES APPARENT ROUGHINESS. IT HAS GOT TO BE IT SO PLEASE LET THIS GEM BE. SO IT CAN HELP BOTH YOU AND ME. TO ME THIS GEM ALWAYS KNOWS HOW TO HELP YOU MAINTAIN BALANCE WITH A FOCUS THAT IS RIGHT. THIS GEM REPRESENTS AN ETERNAL TRUTH AND GUIDING LIGHT. PUT THE TWO TOGETHER AND HEY YOU GOT LIFES INFINITY, TRULY BELIEVE ME, THIS GEM WILL GRASP YOUR HEART JUST FROM A MERE GLIMPSE. THEN WHEN YOU TAKE THIS GEM AND HOLD IT IN THE PALM OF YOUR HAND THE WARMTH LETS YOU KNOW YOU HAVE A GEM STONE FROM THE DEEPEST DEPTHS OF GOD'S EARTH - ITS GLEAM TOLD ME IT'S MY GEM AND ITS HERE TO STAY. AND TOGETHER ME AND THIS GEM WE WILL BE FOR AN ETERNITY. WELL WE ALL CAN ADD HOPEFULLY - THE DEDUCTION IS WHAT IS IMPORTANT. THIS GEM IS GENUINE.
AND ITS LOVING VIBES WERE MADE IN HEAVEN.
DON'T TELL ME ANYTHING DIFFERENT
CAUSE I KNOW THIS GEM IS MINE.

The Sacrificial Confidante

Today I Am… Tranquil
  I Am… Joy
    I Am… Determination

Today I Am LIBERATION
  Yesterday I Was…
        I Was…
          I Was…
I Am Always A Devotee OF The CREATOR…
    THE CREATOR… GOD.
Today I Am… ATTAINMENT

Rightly I Am <u>CONCENTRATING</u> …
 Rightly I Am… MINDFUL of All,
    And of the ALL-IN-ALL

Rightly Viewing… Rightly… I Am Thinking
  I Am Diligent… I AM with Action…
  Rightly Speech, Rightly Livelihood.

<u>TRANSCENDENTAL</u>!!!
    Rightly!
I AM… I AM… DEVOTIONAL
  TODAY I AM… BUDDHA, BRAHMA…
    TOMORROW I WILL BE…
    I WILL BE… ABSOLUTE!

Excerpts From Serenaded Media Style

This morning I awoke earlier than usual.

I went to the back door, opened it. The weather seemed brisk.

I breathed in the cold air. Aagh! The feeling of winter setting in. The fall fading away.

I turned on the heat to get the coldness out of the house before awakening my wee little ones.

I turned on the radio to 104.1 jazz. His favorite. Mine too. Then I put on the album unfinished symphony by Schubert. My mother loved orchestra music... I listened and tears started flowing... I remembered his touch, and he calling me dear, and kid-o, and Huff, and saying yes ma'am in answer to some of my statements.

He did what.

He serenaded me media style.

I was out of the trance state now.

I would slumber off into a deep sleep.

During moments I would awaken to watch the TV.

I could hear him through the TV news cast.

He'd sing to me...

He would.

Yes he would.

He'd play songs on the radio... Some kind of lady...
> Good love.
> My baby.
> You are all I need...
> You are once twice "three" times a lady, I love you... Lionel Richie...

Now for what did he do that to me, media style, and there I was. He continued you shared my dreams, my joys, my pains, you made my life worth living for. If I had to live my life over again, I'd spend each and every moment with you. You are once, twice, three times a lady.. I love you.

Can you just hear him... can you, can you. Gosh! his voice is mellow, warm, sensational...

Excerpts From Serenaded Media Style, Continued

… Thee debonair ontological guy in my life… he serenaded, like no other woman

would ever be… right into the palms of his hand… the heart that he grasped the three years ago

he locked into his hand, never to let it go.

He continued… When we are together the moments I cherish with every beat of my heart.. to touch…

to hold you… to feel you… there is nothing to keep us apart.

He serenaded me media style…

On the TV he would tell me what time he would arrive home…

The soap operas were the script to my (our) life.

It seemed as if body guards surrounded me where ever I went. His body guards… I began to play the

hand I was dealt. The Ace's, Spades, Kings, and Joker.

It seemed as if helicopters were flying over my house, when he couldn't reach me telepathically,

Then I would fall into a slumber again… In my sleep he would awaken me and then all of the sudden

we were exchanging vows.

My wedding

… our wedding… My Big Wedding… It was beautiful, everyone was there. Everyone… the entire City

Hall, and all the fraternities, sororities everyone, everyone you could imagine.

The Pope, The Archbishop, The President… The Politicians, Doctors, Lawyers… Secret Orders, The

Judges.

He is debonair, elegant, suave, smooth… peaceful, gentle… kind, caring in his very own way.

Perfect harmony.

A red bird, a bluebird, a dove, a butterfly flew into my yard and perched.. These a symbol of his kingdom

Indicating that I am his love, today, and forever.

Excerpts From Serenaded Media Style, Continued

I could hear my words as I responded to him, you are all that I want, all that you are, ever have been,

and all that you are going to be. Right into his arms, I was serenaded...

Our vows... Straight from the Bible.

Let him kiss me with the kisses of his mouth: for thy love is better than wine.
I sleep, but my heart waketh: it is the voice of my beloved that knocketh, saying. Open to me,
my sister, my love, my dove.

I opened to my beloved; but my beloved had withdrawn himself, and was gone: my soul failed
when he spoke: I sought him, I could not find him; I called him, but he gave me no answer.
If ye find my beloved, that ye tell him, that I am sick of love.
His mouth is most sweet yea, he is altogether lovely. This is my beloved, and this is my friend.
I am my beloved's, and my beloved is mine: he feedeth among the lilies.

My dove, my undefiled is but one. She is She.

He continued... as I lay outstretched in his arms... He breathing into my ear, words that were
bringing me out of the deep slumber...

Who is she that looketh forth as the morning, fair as the moon, clear as the sun, and terrible as an army
with banners

My eyes opened a little... I peeked... I looked up, his broad shoulders, his long arms holding me.
I saw the sun and its glittering shimmering rays, I saw the moon in vastness of greyish white
with hints of blue...

He pulled me closer into his chest, and said She is She, my beloved, she is here to be with me for
an eternity.

I said to myself, not yet able to speak... struggling to talk... I am my beloved's, and his desire is
toward me.

Finally, he breathed again into me, and we both began to speak, the words flowing eloquently:

Our eyes entranced in each others, my arms tightly around his neck, he continuing to hold me, knowing

that the weeks I laid in a trance left me limp and unable to stand with balance.

Come, my beloved, let us go forth into the field; let us lodge in the villages.

Let us get up early to the vineyards; let us see if the vine flourish, whether the tender grape appear,

and the pomegranates bud forth: there will I give thee my loves.

Many waters cannot quench love, neither can the floods drown it.

Excerpts From Serenaded Media Style, Continued

Hurry (make haste) my beloveth, and be thou like to a roe or to a young hart upon the mountains of spices I thought to myself… now… I remember something about this… then my mind retrospectively went back to the beginning, to the year we first met, and then how we sat mesmerized looking at each other, both smiling, as if to say finally we meet, and this is destined to be never to part again. You could feel the emotions… emotionally you an epic of feelings…

Months have gone by, I thought… as I continued to listen to

"Unfinished Symphony", I said to myself… we married in the astral state… I remember that, and then he serenaded me media style. He did. Thee Debonair Ontological Guy in my life, he held my attention byway of media while I was recuperating from the hypnotic trance. It seemed as if friends of his reported current events, and then would interject scenarios relating to us. I said now if this ain't serenading then what is.

I could feel him holding my hand, I could see that smile, and the gleam in his eyes… I could hear him talking to me smoothly, caressing my every thought… I was destined to remain whole. He was not going to have it any other way. He was not going to lose me again. I was about to slip away into the ether, into what some understand as the heavens. I was no longer going to be a member of this earthly plane. It seems as if there was an instantaneous reincarnation. It was not time for me to leave. He knew this He knows that we are earthly bound.

Slumbering off into a deep sleep, he would breath his female t into me. His female rib, taken from him, he put it into me. All of us are created he an she, female and male. I came this time in dominate female form.

The essence of me is finite female. It was not yet time for me to leave this earthly plane. He made me whole. I was once again whole. Only I have no brain. What little gray matter that I once did have was totally depleted during this hypnotic near comatose state. I have no brain… no gray matter. He'd sing to me… Our wedding song… biblical… I go now my love…

Excerpts From Serenaded Media Style, Continued

He is debonair, elegant, suave, smooth… peaceful, gentle…

I held fast to the Heart of Buddha's teachings… Recognizing that we are each person, that we are one

Unit. I recognized that I could not commit to any other understandings. The other understandings exclude.

Even those that purport to be inclusive. There were two forces pulling… the bad.

The good. The bad, however wanting to, could not prevail.

The Heart of Buddha's teaching… recognition, acceptance, embracing, looking deeply, insight, calming.

Is this He. I continue to exercise the eightfold path of the Noble. Right Action, Right View, Right

Mindfulness, Right Concentration, Right Livelihood, Right Thinking, Right Speech, Right Diligence.

I recognized my suffering and the reason(s) for this suffering. It was time for the suffering to transform

into love, and joy. It couldn't though. As I sat thinking, it won't go away not until he embraces me again,

not until once again he looks deeply with insight and realize that it is I thee destined to be in his life.

Liberated From Suffering

She suffered joyfully.
She suffered gracefully.
She is now liberated… free.
Free from the enslavement of body… of mind.
Free from the bondage… of life's entanglements.
She is free from suffering… Liberated…
Enslavement and bondage of this
earthly realm she no more carries.
She is at last happy.
No more pain. No more hurt.
She is liberated fromlife's unhappiness,
lifes unconcerns, life's uncaring
troublesome moments

BE JOYFUL, BE HAPPY, BE CONTENT… FOR SHE IS…

LIBERATED FROM SUFFERING!!

What Can I Do For You

Are His kindly spoken words.
He's asking, "For you is there anything you would like for me to do"
Not about need.
Not about want.
It is all about what you would like for me to do for you.
His kindly spoken words,
Let me know for me, of Him, I can have anything.
"What can I do for you…"
It's all about you.
"My everything."
Are His kindly spoken words.

THE TRANSFIGURATION

IT IS HIM, IT IS HIM... DON'T YOU <u>STILL</u> KNOW...
THE SAME SPIRIT... THE SAME SOUL...
HE COMES WITH MANY DIFFERENT FACES AND SEEMINGLY
MANY DIFFERENT VOCAL TONES. **TRANSFIGURING...**
THROUGH IT ALL. EACH TIME I KNOW IT'S HIM... HIS SPIRIT
AND SOUL... TRAVELING ALL AROUND INSIDE AND OUTSIDE...
THE SPIRITUAL AND PHYSICAL REALM... DON'T YOU KNOW
HIM... LIKE THE <u>WHITE DOVE</u> HE MOUNTS UP!
SPIRITUAL, ETHERICAL, PHYSICAL... HE'S THE SAME.
MASCULINED YET MEEK, KIND, CONSIDERATE, HUMBLE...
A GENTLE SPIRIT... <u>I KNOW HIM</u>!!!
FOR HEART TO HEART OUR SPIRITS ARE JOINED – NOT
ESTRANGED TO EITHER – AJOINED FOR AN ETERNITY...
FROM ALPHA (THE BEGINNING) TO OMEGA (THE END),
WE'VE KNOWN EACH OTHER...
AT LAST FOREVER WE ARE TO BE...
OUR SPIRITS EMERGE... FINALLY... ON THIS PHYSICAL PLANE,
DO YOU HEAR ME!

REVISION OF...

HE AND ME

AND THERE HE STOOD! WE STOOD, WE STOOD!!
his back turned towards me...
I LIFTED MY HAND!
     Gently on his Shoulder I placed it.
HIS SHOULDERS – MASCULINED, STRONG,
IN AN UPRIGHT POSITION...
          HE TURNED QUIETLY AROUND...
OUR SOULS TOUCHED THE DEEPEST DEPTH OF
EACH.
AND WE STARED... THERE WE STOOD LOOKING
AT EACH OTHER... OUR EYES, OUR VIBRATIONS
CONNECTED... AS IF WE KNEW... OUR HEARTS...
INTERLOCKED... NEVER TO PART... AT LAST TRUE
LOVE IS FOUND...

     KID-O

Revision of...

D
  E
    A
     R

He calls me!
How Sincere... The Sounding...
  When He Calls Me DEAR
I know we are near...
  He called me DEAR... From Him will I again Hear...
Dear... He Calls Me!

<u>Kindred Spirits</u>

So many things do we have in common
Wow! what kindred spirits are we...
The days spent in deepest thought
our spirits roaming here to fore, from
here to there
    only together we are
    kindred spirits is what keeps us alive
    and the flame burning that will not ever die.
    At last kindred spirits we are to be from this day
    an eternity.

QUEENS OF SHEBA

QUEENS OF SHEBA…RISE UP!
WISE, PURE, CHASTE, BEAUTY SO SUBLIME…DIVINE…
THEY CAME TO TEST THE KINGS OF SOLOMON.
ONLY THE APPOINTED ONES PASS THE TESTS THAT ARE PRESENTED.
SPECIFICALLY FOR TWO:
THE APPOINTED QUEEN SHEBA AND THE APPOINTED KING SOLOMON
UNITE.
SO IT IS, SO BE IT.
UNITED THEY ARE THE QUEEN SHEBA AND THE KING SOLOMON AS
APPOINTED TO BE.
QUEEN SHEBA CAN CAUSE A BUTTERFLY TO FLUTTER OR NOT.
SHE COMMANDS THE ANT & BEE TO BUILD KINGDOMS YET TO BE SEEN.
HEAR, SEE, SAY, AND SMELL WHAT OTHERS CANNOT, DOES SHE…
WISE AS CAN BE…
KING SOLOMON IS AS WISE AS SHE…
ALL THE GIFTS ARE NOT BUT TO SHOW APPRECIATION TO THE KING FOR NOT
YIELDING TO TEMPTATION.
THE APPOINTED KING SOLOMON HAS ENTERED.
NO MORE TESTS MUST SHE PRESENT.
THE DESTINED DAY HAS COME FOR, SPECIFICALLY TWO:
THE QUEEN SHEBA AND THE KING SOLOMON TO BE.

A MARRIAGE MADE IN HEAVEN

IN LOVE WITH HIM. HE WITH ME.
I LOVE HIM. HE LOVES ME.
A MARRIAGE MADE IN HEAVEN.
"SACREDLY".
WHAT IS BEGOTTEN IN HEAVEN.
WILL BE BEGOTTEN ON EARTH.
THERE IS NO OTHER WAY IT SHALL BE.
I AWAIT PATIENTLY, FOR THIS EMOTION (EARTHLY
MOTION), DAY TO COME.
ANXIOUS FREE.
IN LOVE WITH HIM. HE WITH ME.
I REMAIN WITH SELF CONTROL.
ANXIOUS OF NOTHING!!

"Trials are test that tempt us and as we resist the temptation we are purified, purged."

"SELF DEFENSE"

"Don't open your mouth…", "keep it shut…". "May I ask why…?"
"No, just don't say a thing…" like a damn thing…". "…Okay…".
"That way people (I mean nobody, no one) will misunderstand or misinterpret what you say…, or who you are…". "…Okay…".
"Cause some kind of way who you are, and what you say isn't heard by others correctly…". "…Okay…". "You know it gets twisted and turned all the wrong ways."
"You're joking ain't ya'?" "May I ask why" "I mean, I haven't <u>knowingly</u> gossiped, slandered, spread lies or unjustly spoken an untruth or <u>knowingly</u> done anything to do mental, emotional, or physical harm." "Therefore, again May I ask why?"
"No, don't ask why, don't say a thing…", "don't ask a thing…, like a damn thing…"
"Well, even if they do misunderstand or misinterpret Who I Am, and what I say…"
"Firstly, I Am That I Am." "Secondly, let me ask this: WHATEVER HAPPENED TO MY FIRST AMENDMENT - RIGHT."
"THE FIRST AMENDMENT". <u>BE</u> <u>QUIET</u> <u>DON"T</u> <u>SPEAK</u>
"You know Freedom of Speech?" "You Just Keep Going On and On and On".
"…There you go…" "I said keep your mouth shut…" "<u>CAN'T</u> <u>YOU</u> <u>HEAR</u>."
"I said don't say a thing, don't ask a thing…like a damn thing…cause no one likes you…, cause you are to damn smart <u>AN</u> <u>INDIVIDUAL</u>." <u>CAN'T</u> <u>YOU</u> <u>HEAR</u>."
"mm"! "…Okay…". "I'll go have my hearing checked." "Why"? "Why"? "I won't ask".
"I'm damned if I do - I'm Damned if I don't". "DON'T ASK <u>WHY</u>!"

PRESIDENT ...

President of the United States.
A Leader of the World.
So much responsibility does he bear.

The economy, environmental control, affirmative action, peace not war -
Between countries, adequate child care, health costs, decent jobs, housing,
A good education, and fair taxes for us all.

Let's balance this budget sensibly.
Prayerfully: with his family (wife and child) at his side, for all humankind he
Serves his country dutifully.

There is only one race, understand this please…one race, one GOD, with
Many different ways of life (religion)…makes sense to me.

The President's concerns are manifold. Let him put it all - he will - in
Comprehensible order…Another "New Deal", if you will.

Don't want to force anyone, can't we agree willingly.

Working congenially (with him) seems to be the clue, instead some politicians
Pull from him divisively… unconcerned… This anyone can discern.

There are those who want to harm and kill, with causes of no substantive
Justification.

I ain't got what he got, he got what I ain't got.
Got… how did he get all that got…
Universal Love and Peace is the cure for all these ills.

Clinton holds his head up high, always giving reverence to the Creator of
us all. His wings out flapped ready to be guided by the Almighty Good.

Let us keep everything in proper context please… what seems literal may not
Be - actually.
Don't go analyzing and assessing what he/she has said, your mind will
Surely roam where it should not be.

The President's job is arduous though he continues with dignity.
His concern for his country and the world is always foremost on his mind.
Let the President serve his country, as this is what he is called to do…
He receives his guidance from the heavenly hosts… permitted to go
Forth with strength… assuredly.

Ansley

I know your mother and father are so very happy and thankful, and so are all your family and friends. As your parents and cousin Kameelah, and other attendees, watch you walk down the aisle, receive that High School Degree, and the tossing of the tassel I can see the tears of joy streaming from their faces, hooray, hooray, you did it Ansley, despite the challenges, Ansley you are victorious. Hugs-Kisses from ME and MyThree (cousins Kassinda, Kameelah, Dennis II). Ansley, AaUntee is so so PROUD and MY chest is poked out big time.

Note to Ansley: Congratulations MY Niece, The Honorable and Degree Conferred Upon, Ansley Lauren Copeland. Ansley, You Shall be encouraged and motivated to continue collegiately, these inbetween milestones are stepping stones that have prepared you for higher academia pursuits. AaUntee is there in spirit.   Love From AaUntee Nece

Keyanna

You are graced with joy and intelligence. Your smile and happiness are felt where ever you appear. You will forever be surrounded with love. You withstood challenges and remained firmly grounded! Growing up your bubbly spirit would bring instantaneous happiness to all of US! Keyanna, you are victorious! Hugs-Kisses from ME and MyThree (cousins Kassinda, Kameelah, Dennis II). You received your high school degree with dignified assurance! The doors of college await you – I know you will excell in college and in your chosen degreed field! Keyanna, you are loved deeply! Hold Your Head Up High, Strut Across That Stage, Hold Your Degree Up High! Toss That Tassel!
       Love From AaUntee Nece

I, Cassandra Huff, Played An Integral Parental Role And Helped Raise MY nephew [Wagner] and MY Three nieces [Nakeah, Ansley and Keyanna]

A Tribute to Mothers:

THE JOYS OF MOTHERHOOD CAN WORDS
EVEN DESCRIBE ... WE ARE EVERY WOMAN ...
THE CHILD LAYING CLOSELY AT MOTHER'S BREAST ...
THE CHILDREN ...
OUR CHILDREN ...
HOW WONDERFUL ARE THEY ...
SMILING, LAUGHING, BABBLING, CRYING ... OUR CHILDREN ... THE JOYS OF
MOTHERHOOD ....
THE WARMTH,
THE CARE,
THE CONCERN ... FOR OUR BABIES, FROM BIRTH THROUGH ALL OF LIFE'S GROWTH
STAGES .... LIFES PHASES ....
THE ETERNAL BOND OF A CHILD AND A MOTHER ..
MOTHERS FEELING LOVED, NEEDED, WANTED.
THE ETERNAL LOVE OF MOTHERS ...
OH MY GOSH CAN WORDS EVEN DESCRIBE ..
THE JOYS OF MOTHERHOOD.
CASSANDRA HUFF
4-6-99

... SISTERS WE ARE ...

WE ARE WE ... WE BE WE ...

WE ARE SISTERS, FEMALE, WOMAN ... SHE ... WE ARE WE ... SISTERS WE ARE ...

... WE BE WE ...

FROM EVERYWHERE, GLOBALLY ... BLACK, WHITE, BROWN ... WE ARE SISTERS ...

... WE BE WE ...

NO MATTER THE CULTURE, THE RACE, THE ETHNICITY, INDOCTRINATION,
RELIGION, CREED, NATIONALITY ... WE ARE WE ... SISTERS WE BE ...

... WE BE WE ...

GOD HAS GIVEN US DIVINE PURPOSE, AN EXACTNESS THAT DESCRIBES
WE ... WE ARE SISTERS ... UNITED ... SO IT BE ... SISTERS ARE WE ...
... EXACTNESS ... EXACTLY ...

... WE BE WE ... SISTERS ARE WE ... WE ...

WE ARE SISTERS!

... WE BE WE ...

... SISTERS WE ARE ...

CASSANDRA HUFF

DECATUR, PANTHERSVILLE, DeKALB COUNTY GEORGIA

HEALTHINESS

Healthiness is principal ["first in order of importance; main"] to maintaining an actuality of overall well being! Under the protected transformation of mental-emotional preparedness of mind body and soul healing is a limitlessly powerful principal to breaking psychological barriers.
-1994- Cassandra Huff

I BID EACH AND EVERYONE A SAFE EVOLVEMENT THROUGH THEIR INDIVIDUAL JOURNEY ON THIS EARTHLY PLANE. NO MATTER HOW, OR HOW OFTEN WE COME TOGETHER, TWO OR MORE, OUR JOURNEY CONTINUES TO BE INDIVIDUAL.

In The Words of Chief Red Jacket:
"FRIEND AND BROTHER, IT WAS THE WILL OF THE GREAT SPIRIT THAT WE SHOULD MEET TOGETHER THIS DAY."

LOVINGLY

Cassandra Huff

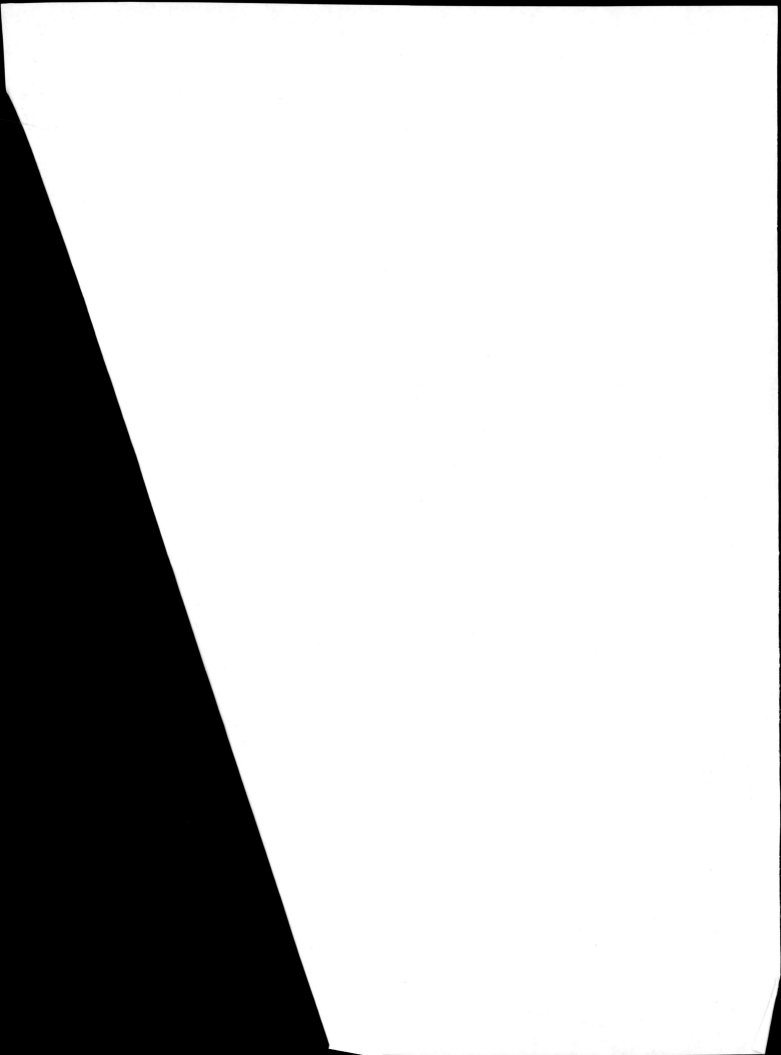

Printed in the United States
by Baker & Taylor Publisher Services